5-Minute
Good Night Stories

PUBLICATIONS INTERNATIONAL, LTD.

Louis Weber, C.E.O.
Publications International, Ltd.
7373 North Cicero Avenue
Lincolnwood, Illinois 60712

www.pubint.com

8 7 6 5 4 3 2 1

ISBN: 0-7853-2726-6

5-Minute Good Night Stories

Contents

Contents

Contents

Contents

Velveteen Rabbit

Illustrated by Phil Bliss and Jim Bliss

Based on the original story by Margery Williams

Adapted by Cynthia Benjamin and Megan Musgrave

One bright Easter morning, a boy woke up to find a wonderful basket waiting for him in his playroom. He was very excited!

The basket was full of jelly beans, chocolate eggs, and marshmallow treats. But the best present of all was his new velveteen rabbit.

The rabbit's coat was soft, and the insides of his ears were shiny satin. He was just the right size for the boy to cuddle. The boy hugged the rabbit close and gave him a kiss on his soft, velvety nose.

The boy stayed in the playroom with the rabbit all day. He didn't play with any of his other toys.

Soon it was dinner time and the boy had to leave his rabbit in the playroom. Once he was gone, the other toys talked to the rabbit.

A shiny robot asked, "What can you do?"

"I don't know," replied the rabbit.

"Well, I can walk back and forth," said the robot. "And someday I am going to be real. Are you?"

The rabbit turned to Old Horse. He was the oldest and wisest toy in the playroom.

"What's real?" asked the rabbit.

Old Horse smiled. "Real is when a child loves you very, very much for a long, long time," he replied. "It's when he loves you so much that your shiny coat grows dull, and you don't look so new any more."

"Oh, my!" exclaimed the rabbit.

"When you are real you don't care how you look because there is nothing better than being loved," said Old Horse. Just then, the boy came into the playroom.

"Come on, Bunny. It's bedtime," said the boy.

The boy took the rabbit to bed with him and snuggled him close all night long. The rabbit felt warm and cozy.

"This must be what it feels like to be loved," thought the rabbit. "Someday I am going to be real."

One day the boy put the rabbit in his red wagon. "You seem to like that rabbit better than all your other toys," said the boy's mother.

"He's not a toy, he's real," said the boy.

The rabbit was so happy. "The boy really loves me," he thought. "And now I am real."

The boy took the rabbit on a ride. When they got to the woods, the boy left the rabbit to search for treasures.

Two strange creatures came out from behind the trees and hopped toward the rabbit. They had long back legs and brown fur.

"What are you?" one of them asked, wrinkling his nose.

"Why, I'm a rabbit, just like you!" said the velveteen rabbit.

"Then why don't you play with us?" asked the other rabbit, hopping around. "You're not real."

"But I am real. The boy told me so," said the velveteen rabbit. But the rabbits just giggled and hopped away.

After a long time, the velveteen rabbit's fur had worn away from being hugged so much by the boy. Most of his fuzzy nose had been kissed away and his satiny ears had lost their shine. But the rabbit was happy because he knew how much the boy loved him.

One day, though, the boy became sick. He didn't want any of his toys anymore, not even the velveteen rabbit.

The doctor told the boy's parents he needed to go away to the seaside to get better. On the day he left, the boy placed the rabbit under their favorite tree in the woods.

"I want you to remember all the wonderful times we had together, Bunny," said the boy sadly.

When the boy went away, the rabbit became very sad. He became so sad that he began to cry. A real tear slid down his velveteen cheek and fell to the ground.

Suddenly a flower grew out of the place where the rabbit's tear had fallen. Its white petals opened, and out stepped a beautiful fairy.

"Do not cry," said the fairy. "I am the fairy of nursery magic. When toys have been loved by a child as much as the boy loved you, I make them real." And with that, she kissed the velveteen rabbit.

Suddenly the rabbit's nose began to itch. Without thinking, he scratched it with his back leg. "I can move!" he cried.

The rabbit began to hop and leap and jump for joy! "Now I am real!" he laughed. The rabbit hopped into the woods and became friends with the rabbits he had met there long ago.

Many months later, the boy returned to his favorite tree. Suddenly a rabbit hopped out from behind.

"You're my velveteen rabbit, aren't you?" asked the boy. The rabbit blinked at the boy, then hopped off into the woods. The boy smiled and said, "I always knew you were real."

Bridget's New Look

Illustrated by Elena Kucharik

Written by Lisa Harkrader

Lucy Ladybug rushed around her beauty shop, getting ready for her customers. "Today will be my busiest day ever," she said. "Everyone in town will be here. They want to look nice for the ball tonight."

Lucy's customers always asked for exactly what they wanted, and Lucy always made sure she gave them exactly what they asked for. Lucy made sure she had everything she would need.

"Lavender shampoo for Hannah Honeybee," said Lucy. "Christine Cricket's styling gel. And extra-firm hair spray for Greta Grasshopper."

Lucy lined up the bottles and unlocked the door of Lucy's Beauty Shop. Hannah, Christine, and Greta hurried through the doors.

Hannah pointed to a picture in a magazine. "Can you make my hair look like this?" she asked.

"No problem," said Lucy.

"My hair needs to be washed and curled," said Christine.

"Have a seat," said Lucy.

"My hair is a mess!" cried Greta. "I need an inch trimmed off. Can you do something to keep it from getting in my eyes while I'm dancing?"

"Of course," said Lucy.

Lucy sat Hannah, Christine, and Greta down. Then Lucy quickly went to work.

Lucy washed and rolled Christine's hair. Then she cut Hannah's bangs. While Christine sat under the hair dryer, she trimmed an inch off Greta's hair.

Soon Christine's hair was dry. Lucy unrolled it and combed it until it shined.

"Exactly what I wanted," said Christine.

Lucy sprayed Greta's hair with hair spray. Then she tied it back with a bow.

"You always give me exactly what I ask for," said Greta.

Lucy pinned Hannah's hair up onto her head. "Here is your new style," said Lucy. "It's called a beehive."

"Perfect!" said Hannah.

As Christine, Greta, and Hannah admired their hairstyles in the mirror, Betty Beetle hurried into Lucy's Beauty Shop with her daughter, Bridget. They both needed their hair styled for the ball, too.

"Fix my hair the usual way," said Betty.

Lucy washed and curled Betty's hair. Then, she brushed it until the ends flipped up.

"How wonderful!" exclaimed Betty. "You always give me exactly what I want."

Bridget had been very quiet. "What kind of style do you want?" Lucy asked her.

Bridget shrugged. She knew what to do on a pitcher's mound or in a batter's box, but she had never been to Lucy's

shop before. Bridget was a little shy about asking for what she wanted.

"Something nice," said Bridget.

"Something nice it is," said Lucy. "I'll give you the latest style."

Lucy trimmed and curled Bridget's hair. Her hair sprang up in little coils all over her head.

"Adorable!" said Hannah Honeybee.

"Cute!" said Greta Grasshopper.

But Bridget didn't say anything. She just sat very still in her chair.

"Is it what you wanted?" asked Lucy.

Bridget stared down at her sneakers. "Well, not exactly," she mumbled.

"Let's try something else," said Lucy. She combed, teased, and sprayed Bridget's hair, then handed Bridget a mirror.

"Lovely," said Christine Cricket.

"Beautiful," said Bridget's mother. But again, Bridget didn't say anything.

"This isn't what you wanted, either, is it?" asked Lucy.

Bridget shook her head. It wasn't what she wanted.

"Maybe you would like a flip, dear." Betty tried to curl up the ends of Bridget's hair.

"Or a beehive," said Hannah. She piled Bridget's hair on top of her head.

Christine thought Bridget needed styling gel. Greta suggested more hair spray. Everyone told Lucy exactly what they thought Bridget wanted.

Everyone except Bridget. She squirmed in her chair as the other customers fussed over her. They poked and pulled and twisted her hair until finally Bridget yelled, "STOP!"

Bridget looked around the shop. "Nobody knows what I want except me. A beehive is fine for Mrs. Honeybee, but I would look funny wearing one. Mom's hairstyle is nice, but it's not right for me. And I like Miss Cricket's curls and Mrs. Grasshopper's bow, but their hair wouldn't look good on me either." Bridget stopped and took a deep breath.

"I really like ponytails," said Bridget, "but Mom says that they aren't dressy enough for the ball."

Lucy smiled. "Let's just see about that."

Lucy curled Bridget's hair again. She pulled it back in two ponytails and tied a pink ribbon around each one. She handed Bridget a mirror.

Bridget slowly looked into the mirror. "Ponytails!" she cried. "Exactly what I wanted."

Lucy nodded. "Here at Lucy's Beauty Shop, when you ask for what you want, you get what you ask for."

"I never knew how pretty ponytails could be!" said Bridget's mother.

Lucy smiled and waved good-bye to her customers. Then she looked at her watch. "Oh, my! I need to hurry if I'm going to get my own hair fixed in time for the ball. Now, what style do I want?"

Little Red Riding Hood

Illustrated by Wendy Edelson

Adapted by Lisa Harkrader

Once upon a time there was a little rabbit who always wore a bright red cloak with a hood. Her name was Little Red Riding Hood.

One day Little Red Riding Hood and her mother packed a basket full of good things to eat. They filled it with her grandmother's favorite foods, like fresh-picked carrots, orange blossom honey, and homemade breads and tarts.

"Please take this basket straight to your grandmother's house," her mother said.

Little Red Riding Hood nodded her head as her mother

helped her put on the red cloak. Her mother tied a beautiful bow under her chin, as only she could do. Then with a kiss on the forehead, her mother sent Little Red Riding Hood off through the woods to Grandmother's house.

Little Red Riding Hood hadn't gone far when a wolf leaped out from the trees. "Where are you going?" he asked.

"I'm not supposed to talk to strangers," said Little Red Riding Hood.

The wolf looked at her basket. "A picnic?" he asked.

"It's not a picnic," said Little Red Riding Hood as she held the basket close. "It's a basket for my grandmother. Now please excuse me, so I can take it to her."

The wolf sniffed the basket. "No flowers? I would never visit my grandmother without a big bunch of flowers. Perhaps you should stop and pick some. You wouldn't want to let her down."

Little Red Riding Hood thought that was a good idea. She picked buttercups and daisies, while the wolf ran down the path toward her grandmother's house.

Grandmother was rocking in her favorite rocker, mending her favorite apron. She hummed a little tune as she worked, so she didn't hear the door creak open. Grandmother also paid careful attention to her needlework, so she didn't see a big, hairy wolf sneak into the house and into the closet.

"Grrr," snarled the wolf as he sprang from the closet.

"Oh, my!" cried Grandmother.

"You look tasty," said the wolf.

Grandmother jumped up from her chair and knocked over the table. She ran out of that house as fast as she could.

The wolf looked through Grandmother's closet and found her nightcap, gown, and some glasses. He put them on, leaped into bed, and pulled the covers up over his nose.

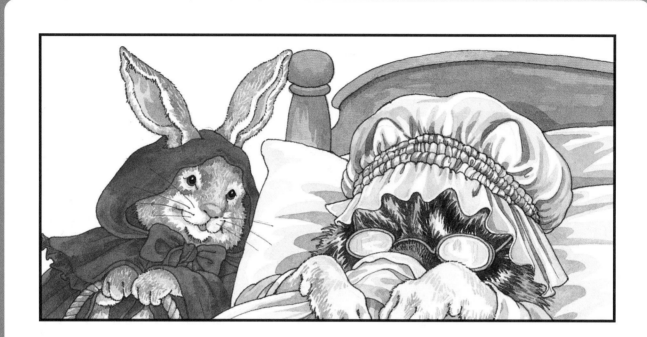

Little Red Riding Hood arrived a few minutes later. "Grandmother, are you home?" she called from the open door. "In here, my little dumpling," said the wolf softly.

Little Red Riding Hood hurried inside. "Grandmother, what big ears you have," she said.

"All the better to hear you with," said the wolf.

Little Red Riding Hood thought her grandmother sounded funny. She leaned in a little closer to hear her better, when she saw the eyes. "Grandmother, what big eyes you have," said Little Red Riding Hood.

"All the better to see you with," said the wolf. Then the wolf slowly pulled down the covers from his face.

"But Grandmother," said Little Red Riding Hood, "what big teeth you have."

"All the better to eat you with," growled the wolf as he jumped off the bed.

"You're not my grandmother!" said Little Red Riding Hood. "Why, you're the big, bad wolf from the forest! What have you done with my grandmother?"

The wolf chuckled. "You'll never find out," he said.

"That's what you think," said someone behind them.

Little Red Riding Hood and the wolf looked up. There was Grandmother, and she was standing in the doorway with a big, strong lumberjack!

The wolf chuckled again. "One old lumberjack can't catch a quick and smart wolf like me."

The wolf leaped toward the bedroom window. But he didn't get very far.

Little Red Riding Hood grabbed the wolf's tail, while Grandmother snatched up her nightcap and pulled it down over the wolf's eyes.

The lumberjack picked up the wolf and carried him off to the bank of the river. Little Red Riding Hood and her grandmother followed close behind.

The lumberjack set the wolf on a big log. He pushed the log into the water, and the wolf quickly sailed down the river.

"He doesn't look so big in the middle of that wide river," said Grandmother.

"He doesn't look so bad when he's so far away," said Little Red Riding Hood.

"And he doesn't look like he'll be coming back any time soon," said the lumberjack as the wolf floated out of sight.

With the wolf safely gone, everyone went back to the house and enjoyed the food in the basket. As Grandmother sipped some tea, she smiled at Little Red Riding Hood. "You are very brave. And I'm glad I'm your grandmother."

Tiny Train's Big Job

Art Developed by Don Williams

Illustrated by H.R. Russell and Therese Simone Russell

Written by Conor Wolf

Adapted by Lisa Harkrader

Tiny Train chugged into the train house. Night was falling and she wanted to get to bed early. "The quicker I get to sleep," she said, "the quicker morning will come."

Tiny Train backed into the train house beside Diesel Engine and Passenger Engine. Tiny Train was the smallest train in the train yard, so she had the smallest stall.

"But I don't mind," she said. "Tomorrow I get to leave the train yard for the first time. I'll show everyone that small trains can do big things."

Tiny Train drifted off to sleep. All night long she dreamed of the things she would do once she left the train yard. In her dreams she hauled valuable cargo over tall mountains. When she delivered her cargo, the engineer and brakeman cheered.

"Thank you, Tiny Train," they said. "You pulled more boxcars than any other engine in the train yard. We couldn't have done it without you."

Once her cargo was delivered, her dreams took her off on another adventure. This time she was an express train, carrying very important passengers to very important meetings far away.

When she arrived at the station, the passengers cheered and shouted, "Thank you, Tiny Train. That was the fastest trip and the smoothest ride we've ever had. We couldn't have gotten here without you."

Morning came, and Tiny Train woke up early. She rumbled out of the train house, ready to make her dreams come true.

"Toot! Toot!" Tiny Train sounded her whistle and chugged down the tracks out of the train yard. She saw Diesel Engine pulling a heavy load of logs and coal.

"I could pull a load like that," Tiny Train thought to herself. She rolled over to Diesel Engine and blew her whistle again. "I'm here to help," said Tiny Train.

"If you want to help," puffed Diesel Engine, "just stay out of my way. I've got hard work to do."

"I can work hard," said Tiny Train.

"I'm sure you can," said Diesel Engine. "But this job is too big for a little train like you. Run along and find something else to do. Something your size." Diesel Engine chugged on with his heavy load.

Tiny Train frowned. "Small trains can do big things."

She tooted her whistle and chugged off down the tracks. Soon she saw Passenger Engine. Passenger Engine looked so sleek and shiny carrying her important passengers. Tiny Train could see those passengers through the windows. She saw serious-looking business people traveling to meetings. She saw excited families eager to start their vacations. They were all depending on Passenger Engine to get them where they were going.

"They could depend on me, too," Tiny Train thought to herself. She tooted her whistle and sped up to catch Passenger Engine. "I came to help," said Tiny Train.

"You are much too small," said Passenger Engine, "and we are going too fast. You could never keep up."

"Yes, I could," panted Tiny Train. "I'm very dependable."

"Yes, you are," said Passenger Engine, "but this job is too big for a little train like you. Run along and find something else to do. Something your size."

Passenger Engine steamed off down the tracks. Tiny Train huffed and puffed to a stop. "Passenger Engine was going fast," she said, "but I could go fast, too. Small trains can do big things."

Tiny Train tooted her whistle and chugged off down the tracks. Soon she came to the zoo tunnel. A train car was stopped on the tracks. Baby Elephant sat inside the car. Railroad workers and zoo officials were looking at Baby Elephant and scratching their heads.

Tiny Train rolled over to the train car. "What's the matter?" she asked.

"I need to get into the zoo to be with my mother," said Baby Elephant. "But all the train engines are too big to go through such a small tunnel."

Tiny Train looked at the tunnel. "It's small," she said, "but so am I!"

Tiny Train backed up and hooked onto Baby Elephant's train car. She puffed out steam, tooted her whistle, and chugged through the tunnel.

Baby Elephant was so happy she raised her trunk and let out a big trumpeting sound. Mama Elephant was also happy and trumpeted back.

The railroad workers and zoo officials cheered. "Thank you, Tiny Train," they said. "We couldn't have done it without you. You can work here every day. This job is just the right size for you."

The animals all cheered. Tiny Train was very happy.

"This job is the right size for me," Tiny Train said as she chugged down the track, "because small trains can do big things, you know."

Patch's Lucky Star

Illustrated by Loretta Lustig

Written by Catherine McCafferty

Adapted by Brian Conway

Patch was a pretty little turtle who lived by the pond. She was as quiet and careful as a turtle could be. Most turtles her age romped along the shores of the pond all day, but Patch did not.

Patch looked just like any other young turtle she knew, except for one thing. She had a yellow patch on the outside of her shell. Patch was the only turtle on the pond to have such a shell. "It is such an odd shell for a turtle to have," Patch thought to herself.

"It's not odd," Patch's mother would tell her often. "It's just different. It makes you special, Patch."

Patch did not want to be special. She just wanted a normal shell so everyone would stop looking at her patch.

Patch would hide away most of the day among the tall grasses around the pond. Sometimes she would creep and crawl to her favorite spots on the pond, but only when she was sure there was nobody around.

Most days, Patch just tucked herself up inside her shell and stayed there. Patch liked staying inside her shell very much. Inside it was dark and quiet. Inside Patch could be all alone.

Patch didn't have to worry about getting splashed by frogs or being sniffed by the bigger animals that came to drink from her pond. And if any of the other animals were looking at her odd shell, Patch didn't want to see their stares.

Most of all, though, she didn't want to have to look at her own shell. She thought the big yellow patch was terrible. In fact, she thought it made her whole shell look terrible. So Patch stayed inside her shell, where she did not have to see it or anything else.

Patch stayed there and daydreamed the day away. In her thoughts, she would stick her head out proudly and walk in the flower patch. Patch would go from flower to flower like a bee and smell the wonderful smells.

From the darkness of her shell, Patch also imagined she had great adventures. She saw herself zipping and diving from shore to shore like a dragonfly.

One day, Diamond and Snapper walked by Patch's hiding place. She hoped the two young turtles would not notice her, but they came up and tapped on her shell.

"Patch!" they called. "Come exploring with us."

Patch stayed very still in her shell. Soon they went away.

Patch pretended she went exploring with them. She thought about finding a cool, shady place where she could slide down a great big log and splash into the pond.

Later that day, Patch heard her mother's voice outside her shell. Poking her head out, Patch was surprised to see Diamond and Snapper's mother there, too.

"Have you seen Diamond or Snapper?" Patch's mother asked. "They've been gone for hours."

"They went exploring," Patch told her.

Diamond and Snapper's mother shook her head. "We'll have to go looking for those two," she said. "It's getting dark."

"You stay here, Patch," her mother said. "We don't need another lost turtle."

Patch shivered, glad she had stayed inside her shell. She thought it must be scary to be lost on the pond at night. Then she saw that the stars were starting to glitter in the dark sky.

"If only my shell could shine as brightly as the stars," she thought aloud, "I wouldn't mind my patch so much."

As Patch sighed, she heard Diamond and Snapper calling for their mother. Their mother called back, relieved to hear their voices again. Their voices were coming closer to Patch's place on the shore.

Patch quickly ducked back into her shell. Soon it seemed that all the turtles were just outside, huddled around her. Everyone was talking all at once.

"We kept going in circles," Snapper said.

"Everything looked the same in the dark," added Diamond. "But then we saw Patch's bright yellow patch all the way across the pond."

"We followed it all the way back!" said Snapper.

"Thank goodness for that patch!" their mother said.

"If you ever get lost again," Diamond and Snapper's mother said, "be sure you follow the North Star."

She pointed up to the brightest star in the sky.

"We don't need the North Star," Snapper said. "We've got our own star right here on the shore!"

"And it's the brightest star on the pond, that's for sure!" said Diamond.

"Patch," her mother said, "they're talking about your special shell."

Patch was so happy, her shell couldn't hold her. She popped out and looked back at her patch. In the moonlight, it did shine brightly!

Tomorrow Patch would come out again to see just how much it really did shine. She hoped her star would shine all the time.

Speedy Colt

Illustrated by Erin Mauterer

Title Page Illustrated by Lyn Martin

Written by Catherine McCafferty

Adapted by Sarah Toast

Speedy was a lively colt. He lived on a farm with many horses. Speedy's whole family lived there and so did other families with their little colts.

Speedy and his friends were born in the early spring. They enjoyed their very first summer together. The colts had nothing much to do but play all day in the fields.

Speedy had a best friend named Lightning. Speedy and Lightning were growing bigger and stronger every day.

"Come on, Lightning!" said Speedy. "Let's play chase with the others."

All the colts tore around the fields, chasing each other, chasing the butterflies, and chasing the wind. They loved to play chase together.

Speedy and Lightning were the fastest little colts on the farm. They raced way ahead of the other colts. Then they circled back to their friends and played chase with them some more.

One day Speedy's mother said to him, "You seem to be enjoying yourself and your friends. I am glad to see you play with them all day in the sunshine. You have grown into a big, strong colt."

"Thank you, Mother," said Speedy. "My best friend Lightning is as fast as I am!"

Speedy started off toward the field where Lightning was waiting for him. But his mother called after him.

"Not so fast, Speedy," said his mother. "I have something important to talk to you about."

Speedy came back to his mother. "Sorry, Mother," he said. Speedy waited to hear what she had to say.

"Son," said his mother, "your grandfather would like to spend some time with you and show you around the woods."

"But Mom," said Speedy, "Grandpa is so slow! He doesn't play chase, and he can't race! He's not much fun."

"Your grandfather may be slow, but that doesn't mean he isn't fun," said Speedy's mother. "And he would enjoy your company."

"I really love Grandpa," said Speedy. "I want him to be happy. I promise I'll visit with him tomorrow."

"That would be very nice, Speedy," said his mother.

Speedy ran off to the path. Lightning and the other colts were waiting for him there. First they played chase together. Then Speedy and Lightning raced each other. Speedy won the first race, and Lightning won the second one.

The next day, Speedy forgot about his promise to his mother. He and his friends played all day without a care, until Speedy and Lightning's big race.

Speedy and Lightning raced each other like always. But this time, they ran clear to the edge of the field, which is where the woods began.

Speedy remembered that his grandfather wanted to show him the woods. "I will keep my promise tomorrow!" Speedy thought to himself. "Today I'll explore the woods with Lightning." But Lightning didn't want to go any further.

"Then I'll go on my own," Speedy said as he trotted off.

"Come back," Lightning called. "You'll get lost!"

"No, I won't," shouted Speedy in reply. "I'll be alright. See you back at the stable!"

At first Speedy whinnied with joy as he trotted further into the woods down the wide path. But he ran so fast that he was soon very far from where he had been before.

One wide path joined another. Speedy wasn't sure which way to turn to get back to the field.

First he tried one path, then he tried another. No matter which way he tried, he was still in the woods.

Speedy began to get scared. Finally he stood still and tried not to cry. Speedy didn't know when he would see his mother and his grandfather again.

"They must be very worried," Speedy thought to himself. As he hung his head down, a tear ran down his cheek and fell onto the path below.

Just then Speedy heard the steady clip-clop of a horse walking down the path. He looked up and was instantly filled with relief. It was his grandfather walking toward him!

"Grandpa!" said Speedy. "I was lost, but you found me!"

"Good to see you," said his grandfather. "Lightning came to tell me that he waited for you at the edge of the woods for a long time. I just thought I'd come and meet you!"

"Why aren't you lost, too?" asked Speedy.

"I know every path on the farm and in these woods," said his grandfather, as they walked out together. "I've had many years to get to know the place. Perhaps I can take you and Lightning on a long walk through the woods tomorrow."

"That's great!" said Speedy. "I guess there's more to life than running around, huh, Grandpa?"

"Sometimes you just need to slow down," said his grandfather, "and spend more time with your family."

Bitsy's Big Day

Illustrated by Steve Boswick

Written by Catherine McCafferty

Bitsy Spider hurried down the path. Her bag was full of Spider Deliveries, and she had to deliver them fast! The Crickets, her very favorite band, were in town today. Bitsy wanted to try out for the band. If they asked her to join, she could play music all the time!

"Spider Delivery for Mr. Jeeter Bug!" Bitsy called at her first mailbox.

"Hi, Bitsy!" said Jeeter. "Hooray! It's two letters from the Green Glowworm Fan Club! I joined last week!"

Bitsy smiled as Jeeter jumped up and down. "Enjoy your letters!" she said.

As Bitsy turned to go, Jeeter asked, "Do you have time for a game of Tick Gnat Toe? Do you, Bitsy? Huh? Do you?"

Bitsy wanted to get through all her Spider Deliveries. But Jeeter looked so hopeful.

"Anything for a friend," she said. "Let's make it quick!"

They played a very fast and fun game. "Thanks!" said Jeeter as Bitsy left.

Bitsy would have to deliver faster to make up for that game stop. She hurried along, when she heard a horn honking.

"Morning, Bitsy," said Buzz Bee.

"Good morning," she replied.

"You wouldn't have any oil, would you? Lady Bug's car broke down. She wants me to fix it before the Garden Bug meeting is over. And I can't leave the car to go back to the garage."

Bitsy was in a big hurry. "But one more stop won't hurt," she thought.

"Anything for a friend," she said. Bitsy brought back the oil and poured it into Lady Bug's engine.

"You are a friend indeed," said Buzz. He honked the car horn in salute as Bitsy waved good-bye.

Bitsy ran down the road to Sue Fly's house. Now she had to make up for a game stop and an oil stop!

Sue Fly was snoring very soundly when Bitsy arrived. Bitsy quietly pulled a pair of new glasses from her bag when Sue's old glasses fell off her chair.

Cr-r-rack-k-k! Pieces of glass scattered all over the floor. Sue woke up. "What happened?"

"Don't get up, Sue!" called Bitsy. She got a damp cloth and wiped up the glass. Bitsy didn't want Sue to cut herself.

"My eyes aren't what they used to be," said Sue. She put on her new glasses. "Thank you, Bitsy."

"Anything for a friend," Bitsy replied. She turned to leave and looked at the sun.

"Oh, dear!" Bitsy said to herself. "It's afternoon already!"

On her way to Lady Bug's house, Bitsy saw the Garden Bug meeting. "I can give Lady Bug's letters to her now," Bitsy thought to herself.

"Thank you," said Lady Bug. "Could I ask you a favor?"

Bitsy knew she had many more Spider Deliveries to make. But she thought she could squeeze in one little favor.

"I left my pie in the car," said Lady Bug. "Do you think you could make a special Spider Delivery for me?"

"Anything for a friend," she said. Bitsy ran to Lady Bug's car and got the pie. But she couldn't run with the pie, so she walked back.

The Garden Bugs were glad to see their pie. Bitsy was happy to deliver it. But she was worried about her other deliveries. It was getting late.

"I'll take a shortcut through this yard," Bitsy said to herself. "But first I need a little rest. All that running made my legs tired."

Bitsy sat on the edge of a spout and sorted her Spider Deliveries. Across the yard, she saw her friend Jeeter Bug. He was trying to tell her something, but she couldn't hear him.

Whoosh-h-h! Water gushed out of the spout and washed Bitsy across the yard.

"My Spider Deliveries!" cried Bitsy. "I'll never get them dried and delivered in time. And I'll never get to try out for The Crickets!"

Jeeter Bug patted Bitsy on the shoulder. "Don't worry, Bitsy," he said. "I'll get help."

Soon, Jeeter Bug, Buzz Bee, Lady Bug, and Sue Fly pulled up in Lady Bug's car. "You helped us," said Lady Bug. "Now we'll help you."

Everyone held out the letters to dry, as Lady Bug drove Bitsy along her route. The letters dried quickly and Bitsy finished her deliveries just in time.

"That was a lot of fun!" said Bitsy's friends. "Now let's go to the tryout!"

At the tryout, Bitsy played her song. The Crickets jumped in to play along. When they were done, The Crickets said, "You have got to join us!"

"I'd love to," said Bitsy, "but who will take over my Spider Delivery route?"

"We will!" her friends shouted. "But could we ask you a little favor? Will you play us another song?"

"Anything for my friends," she said.

Paper Route Puppy

Illustrated by Thomas Gianni

Written by Catherine McCafferty

Max wheeled his bicycle slowly down the street. He counted the newspapers in his basket. There were enough of them. He counted the money in his pocket. There wasn't enough of it.

Today was supposed to be Puppy Day. Max had planned to buy a puppy at Mr. Ross's pet shop, which was the last stop on his route. He had saved his paper route money for months now. In fact, Max had started delivering papers so he could save for a puppy.

Max thought he had enough money this morning. But then his mother said, "Don't forget to buy a leash and a collar and dog food. A puppy needs those things."

Max knew his mother was right. But he was tired of waiting for his puppy.

Max delivered his first paper at Anatelli's Music Store. Mr. and Mrs. Anatelli could play every instrument in the store, even the drums!

"Is today Puppy Day, Max?" called Mr. Anatelli.

Max shook his head. "Maybe next month." He told Mr. and Mrs. Anatelli what his mother had said.

Mrs. Anatelli patted Max on the arm. Then she hurried out of the shop.

"Maybe I won't get a puppy at all," Max said. He picked up a drumstick and tapped on the drums. Max already had enough money to pay for lessons. And if he learned to play, he could be in the school band! But as he asked Mr. Anatelli about lessons, Mrs. Anatelli came back.

"No, Max," said Mrs. Anatelli. "Wait and get your puppy. His barking will be music to your ears. You could call him Drummer."

She handed Max a package. "Please take this to Mr. Ross." Max looked at the drums one last time, then went on his way.

At Goldman's Book Nook, Max spotted a new book. It told all about a sunken pirate ship that had just been discovered. There were pictures of gold coins, cannon balls, and even the ship's bell!

Max counted his money. He had enough for the book. "I'd like to buy this book, please," said Max.

"Oh, no, Max, I'm sorry," Mrs. Goldman said. "I can't sell you that. It's the only copy I have. Besides, I thought today was Puppy Day."

"I have to wait another month for a puppy," said Max. "I just thought I could have this book now." Max put the book down. Nothing was going his way today.

"Well, you wait for your puppy. You could call him Pirate." Mrs. Goldman handed Max a package. "Please give this to Mr. Ross when you see him."

Max put her package in with his papers. He got on his bike and pedaled to his next stop.

At Mrs. Garcia's Candy Shop, Max knew for sure what he would buy. He would get enough candy to stock his tree house until next Halloween.

When Max tried to go into the shop, Mrs. Garcia wouldn't let him in. She didn't want to sell Max any candy.

"A puppy's company will be sweeter than all the candy in my shop. You could even call him Candy!" she laughed.

Max still wanted to go inside, but Mrs. Garcia handed him a package. "Please take this next door to Mr. Ross."

Max wheeled his bicycle to Mr. Ross's door. Puppies and dogs yipped and danced inside. The parrot called, "Hello!"

"I can't get a puppy today, Mr. Ross," Max said.

"Well, that works out," said Mr. Ross, "because I can't sell you a puppy today."

"Nobody will sell me anything today," Max told him. "Not drum lessons, not books, not candy. And I don't have enough money to buy a puppy."

Mr. Ross smiled. "Well, that works out, too, Max. Your friends bought a puppy for you."

"Surprise!" Mr. and Mrs. Anatelli, Mrs. Goldman, and Mrs. Garcia crowded into the pet shop. Max couldn't believe it. It really was Puppy Day after all!

"All you have to buy is a collar, a leash, and some dog food," said Mr. Anatelli. "Now open the packages we gave you."

One by one, Max opened the gifts. There was a dog whistle from Mr. and Mrs. Anatelli, a dog book from Mrs. Goldman, and a dog biscuit from Mrs. Garcia. "Now it's time to pick a puppy," they said.

Max scooped up three puppies. Two of the puppies wiggled out of his arms. But the fluffy white puppy stayed in his arms and even licked his face!

"This is my new puppy!" said Max. "Do you think I should name him Drummer or Pirate or Candy?" His friends didn't know and Max couldn't decide.

"One thing's for sure. I'm very lucky to have friends like you!" Max said. "Hey, that's it! I'll call my puppy Lucky."

Cedar's New Tooth

Illustrated by Jean Pidgeon

Written by Catherine McCafferty

Adapted by Lisa Harkrader

Cedar Squirrel sat up in his nest. *Gr-r-rum-m-mble.* What got him up so early?

Cedar rubbed his eyes and glanced around. His older brothers, Sassafras and Oak, were asleep.

Gr-r-rum-m-mble. Cedar clapped his paws over his tummy. That's why he woke up! His stomach was growling.

"Maybe I can get a little snack," said Cedar as he yawned and stretched.

Then Cedar frowned. "Something is different," he said. "Something isn't right."

Cedar glanced around his nest. It didn't look different. Cedar rustled around in his leafy bed. It didn't look different. Cedar peered at his sleeping brothers. They didn't look different either.

Then Cedar felt what was different. His front tooth, his very best acorn-munching tooth, had fallen out.

"Oh, no!" Cedar cried.

Cedar rushed around the nest, scattering leaves and twigs every which way. He looked in every corner and in every nook and cranny. But the tooth wasn't there.

Cedar even poked his front paw under his sleeping brothers to see if they were lying on anything. But Cedar didn't find his tooth.

"Oak," Cedar whispered. "Please wake up. My tooth, I can't find it anywhere."

Oak, who was usually so wise, just muttered, "Sassafras probably hid it." He rolled over and snuggled under the soft leaves.

Cedar shook his other brother. "Do you know where my tooth is?" But Sassafras continued snoring. Cedar shook him again.

Sassafras buried his head under the leaves. So Cedar shook even harder.

"Sassafras, wake up! I lost my tooth. Did you take it?"

Sassafras opened one eye. "Why would I want your tooth?" he asked. Cedar shrugged his shoulders.

"I'll take your acorns, though," Sassafras mumbled as he closed his eyes. "You won't be able to crack them with one of your teeth missing."

No acorns! Sassafras was right. Without that tooth, Cedar wouldn't be able to crack acorns.

"Maybe I just need to practice," said Cedar.

Cedar hurried over to the pile of acorns they had stored for the winter. One of the acorns had rolled away and was lying in the leaves.

Cedar picked it up. Then he looked at it carefully.

"I'll find a way to crack this," said Cedar. He put the acorn in his mouth. Cedar bit down, but the acorn didn't crack. It just slid out of his mouth.

Cedar tried again and again. But the acorn shell stayed smooth and whole.

"Not even one little crack," moaned Cedar. He went to find his mother.

"Mama!" Cedar called out. "Mama, my tooth."

Cedar ran to her. Then he opened his mouth wide so his mother could see.

"It looks like you've lost one," said his mother. She didn't seem worried.

"But I can't eat acorns without my tooth," said Cedar.

His mother smiled. "Maybe you can't now. But you'll grow a new tooth soon."

"How will I crack acorns until then?" Cedar hung his head.

His mother chuckled. "You'll have to eat something else for a while."

At breakfast Cedar's mouth watered as he looked at the acorns and nuts Oak and Sassafras had. Cedar had a pile of mushy berries.

"I won't wait to get my new tooth," said Cedar. "I'm going to get one now."

"Where do you think you'll find another squirrel tooth?" asked Sassafras.

"I don't know," said Cedar. "But I'll find out."

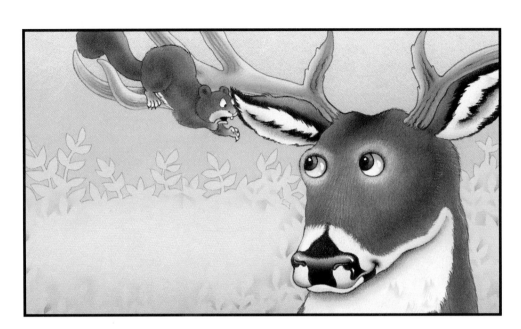

Cedar left his berries. He raced through the woods to find his friend, Buck Deer.

"Buck," he said, "my tooth fell out." Cedar crawled up on Buck's antlers and opened his mouth wide. "Where can I get a new one?"

Buck peered into Cedar's mouth. "There's only one place to get a new squirrel tooth," he said.

Cedar's eyes widened. "Where?"

Buck chuckled. "Inside a squirrel's mouth, of course."

Cedar hung his head and stared at the ground. "Don't be funny," he said.

"I'm not being funny," said Buck. "A new tooth will grow where your old tooth was."

"I know," said Cedar. "But I don't want to wait that long before I can eat acorns again."

Buck looked into Cedar's mouth again. "You won't have to," he said. "Your new one is already coming in."

Cedar felt the spot where his tooth used to be. Near the top, there was a little nub.

"You're right!" Cedar told Buck. "I'm getting a new tooth!"

Cedar leaped around. He twitched his ears and swished his fluffy tail.

"I'll be cracking acorns again in no time!" Cedar shouted.

Gr-r-rum-m-mble. Cedar clapped his paws over his tummy. He had forgotten how hungry he was.

"I guess I'll have to get used to eating berries," said Cedar. He waved good-bye to Buck and happily ran home to have his breakfast.

Bookworm Library

Illustrated by Elena Kucharik

Written by Sarah Toast

Adapted by Lisa Harkrader

Cora Caterpillar rushed through town. When she reached the Bookworm Library, she unlocked the door and hurried inside.

Cora was the head librarian. She had a long list of things to do before the library opened.

Cora read her list. "Number one: straighten shelves."

Cora bustled up and down the rows and rows of bookshelves. She straightened books that were leaning over.

106

Cora also picked up books that had fallen on the floor. She found books that were upside down and put them back the way they belonged.

When she finished, Cora looked at the neat rows of books. "They look like an army of ants," she said proudly, "standing at attention."

Cora read her list again. "Number two: turn on computers."

Cora went to the table of computers. One by one, she pushed the buttons to turn each computer on. One by one, the computers hummed to life.

Cora listened. "They're buzzing like a beehive," she said.

Cora looked at her list again. "Number three: choose two books for story hour." Cora frowned. "This will be hard. I like so many," she said to herself.

It was true. The Bookworm Library had hundreds of great books. How could she choose just two?

Cora thought about the books she loved best. She liked animal stories and funny stories and westerns and poems. Cora snapped her fingers. "I'll read a book of poems about animals and a funny book about a cowboy," she said.

Cora found the books, then looked at the clock. It was time for the library to open.

Cora unlocked the door. Young bugs from all over town raced inside. Sally Spider came with Francine Firefly. Busby Bumblebee brought Wally Waterbug and a little bitty bug, Rollie Roly-Poly.

The little bugs pulled books from the shelves. They piled lots of books on the tables. They laughed and talked and read out loud.

"Oh, my," Cora thought to herself. "How can such little bugs make such a big racket?"

Cora put her finger to her lips. "Sh-sh-sh-sh," she said. Nobody heard her.

"Quiet," whispered Cora. "We can't be noisy in the library." Nobody paid attention.

Cora sighed. She looked at the two books in her arms and smiled. "Does anybody want to hear a story?" Cora called out in a louder voice.

The little bugs looked at each other. "Yes!" they cheered.

The young bugs scrambled over to the story circle. They spread out on the soft carpet and plump pillows.

Cora settled into her big cushy chair and began to read. The little bugs listened to the animal poems and the funny western story.

"I liked the poem about the butterfly and the lion," said Busby Bumblebee.

"I liked the cowboy," said Wally Waterbug.

"I liked the cowboy's horse," said Sally Spider.

Rollie Roly-Poly didn't say anything. He was fast asleep.

Francine Firefly giggled. "Rollie thought we were reading bedtime stories," she said.

"Now it's time to find books to take home," said Cora.

"I want a book about weaving," said Sally Spider.

"I want a book about boats," said Wally Waterbug.

Sally and Wally and Francine and Busby went off to find books. Cora gently shook Rollie Roly-Poly.

"Time to wake up," Cora said. Rollie rubbed his eyes. "Do you want to take a book home?" Cora asked. Rollie nodded sleepily and yawned.

The little bugs all found books. They marched up to Cora's desk to check them out.

Cora wrote each little bug's name on a card in the book. She took out a big rubber stamp and stamped each card.

"You can take these books home to read," Cora said. "You can keep them for two whole weeks."

The little bugs gathered their books. They put them in their bags and filed toward the door.

"Good-bye, Sally," said Cora. "Good-bye, Wally and Busby and Francine." Cora stopped. Where was Rollie?

"Has anyone seen Rollie?" Cora asked the children. Sally and Wally and Busby and Francine shook their heads.

"Help me find him," said Cora.

Cora looked under the tables. Sally looked by the humming computers. Francine and Wally and Busby looked behind the bookshelves. No Rollie.

"Where did he go?" Cora asked.

"The last time I saw him," said Francine, "he was sleeping on a pillow in the story circle."

Cora smiled and hurried to the story circle. There was Rollie, curled up in Cora's big chair, fast asleep.

Cora chuckled. "I guess my bedtime stories really work," she said.

Cora woke Rollie and helped him check out a book. Then she sent the children home.

"I love being a librarian," Cora said. "And I love helping the little bugs of our town."

Little Quack

Illustrated by Kurt Mitchell

Written by Sarah Toast

Adapted by Catherine McCafferty

It was Little Quack's first day on the pond! There were so many new things to see. Little Quack stopped again and again.

"Little Quack, go to the back!" his sisters said. "You're holding up the line."

"OK," said Little Quack.

Little Quack didn't mind going to the back of the line. It gave him more time to explore.

When his family walked through the reeds, Little Quack peeked around them. When his family looked straight ahead, Little Quack looked up at the trees. When his family swam on the water, Little Quack dipped under it. When a creature under the water blew bubbles, Little Quack blew some back.

His family kept paddling along. Little Quack didn't notice that they were swimming away. They didn't seem to notice that Little Quack stayed behind to play.

 When Little Quack popped above water again, his family was nowhere in sight. Little Quack looked around. All the new things at the pond seemed a little scary now. Little Quack would feel better if his family were here. How would he find them?

Little Quack paddled in a slow circle. A strange green animal with a loud, deep voice watched him. As a fly buzzed past, the strange green animal's tongue shot out. *Z-z-zip-p-p!* He caught the fly. Little Quack backed up. What if the green animal caught him?

The green animal laughed as Little Quack back-paddled. "Don't worry, Ducky," the animal said. "I'm a frog. I eat bugs, not ducks."

That made Little Quack feel better. "Hello, Frog," he said. "I'm looking for my family. Have you seen them?"

"I only look for flies, not ducks," croaked Frog. "You should ask Bluebird. She sees everything on the pond."

"Bluebird?" Little Quack said to himself. He wondered if Frog was playing a joke on him. Little Quack had never heard of a bluebird. His mother had some blue feathers, but the rest of her was a lovely brown. Little Quack wished he could see his mother's feathers right now.

"I guess I will keep looking," Little Quack said.

As he paddled along, Little Quack saw some blue feathers. He hurried toward them.

But it was not his mother. It was the bluebird! Little Quack stared at her. She looked so different, but pretty.

"Hello, little one," Bluebird chirped. Her voice was a sweet, lovely song.

"No, my name is Little Quack," the duckling told her.

Bluebird laughed. "Where is your family, Little Quack?" she asked.

"I don't know," said Little Quack. "Frog says that you can help me find them. Do you know where they are?"

"Wait here," said Bluebird. "I'll look."

Bluebird flew off, but was not gone for long. She landed on a cattail by Little Quack.

"Did you find them?" asked Little Quack.

"Your family is just over there," Bluebird said as she pointed with her wing.

Little Quack followed her direction and paddled off. But the shore all looked the same now. Little Quack couldn't tell if he was going in the right direction.

Little Quack looked all around, but he couldn't find his mother and he couldn't see the bluebird. And worst of all, a strange animal was watching him from the shore!

Little Quack backed away. The animal got closer to the water.

"Hi there!" the animal called. "Were you born this spring, too?"

Little Quack stopped. "I was hatched, not born," he said. "Who are you?"

The animal laughed. "I'm Fox Kit."

"Why don't you have feathers?" asked Little Quack.

"Foxes don't have feathers," Fox Kit said. "We have fur."

"Poor Fox Kit," Little Quack thought to himself. "It must be hard not to have feathers."

"Everyone in my family has feathers," said Little Quack. "If you want, we could all give you some. But first I have to find my family."

Fox Kit smiled. He didn't seem so strange anymore. "That's all right," he said. "I think I saw your family on the other side of these cattails."

"Thank you," said Little Quack.

Little Quack swam as fast as he could. He didn't stop to explore, he didn't look up at the trees, and he didn't take a dip under the water. Little Quack went straight to the other side of the cattails, and there was his family!

"Mother!" Little Quack called. He was so happy to see her and his sisters.

His mother lifted her wing and Little Quack swam underneath it. He nuzzled his mother's fine feathers.

"I didn't know where you were," said Little Quack.

"I always knew where you were," his mother said. "I never lost sight of you and I never will. For you are my Little Quack."

Ziggy's Fine Coat

Illustrated by Debbie Pinkney

Written by Catherine McCafferty

Adapted by Megan Musgrave

Ziggy was a handsome young tiger cub who lived in the jungle with his parents. His mother was the most kind and beautiful tigress in all of the jungle, and his father was the most handsome and mighty tiger.

But Ziggy never felt like he fit in. His stripes always made him feel out of place.

One day Ziggy and his father went to the watering hole for a drink. He looked at his reflection in the shiny surface

of the water. All he saw were stripes, stripes, and more stripes.

"Dad, I just don't know what to do about these stripes," said Ziggy sadly. "Yours and Mama's seem to fit you, but mine are just funny-looking."

"Son, you have brighter and bolder zigzag stripes than any other cub in the jungle," said his father. "That's why we named you Ziggy. Don't worry. You'll grow into your stripes one day."

That didn't make Ziggy feel much better. He thought and thought as he wandered through his jungle home.

"There must be some way to get rid of these stripes," Ziggy muttered to himself.

Just then, Ziggy's parrot friend Kiko swooped down from the trees and landed on top of a flower bush. "What's the matter, Ziggy?" asked Kiko.

"I don't want to be striped anymore," Ziggy explained.

Kiko hopped out of the big flower bush. "Maybe these bright red flowers could help," suggested Kiko.

Ziggy stared at the beautiful flowers. Suddenly, he came up with an idea.

"Those flower petals just might do the trick! " he said.

Ziggy carefully plucked some of the flower petals from the bush. Then he licked his coat and pasted the petals all over himself. Soon all of his black stripes were covered.

"Not a stripe in sight!" said Kiko gleefully.

No sooner had Kiko said this, though, than a strong breeze blew through the jungle. The breeze blew all of Ziggy's beautiful flower petals away.

"Oh, no," cried Ziggy. "My big, old stripes are back again."

Just then, Ziggy's monkey friend Maka swung down from a nearby tree. "Why the long face?" asked Maka.

"I'm tired of always being striped. I wish I could find a way to get rid of these silly stripes once and for all," sighed Ziggy.

Maka thought only for a short while. The mischievous monkey was always full of good ideas.

"I have just the thing for you," laughed Maka. "Why don't you paint your stripes with mud?"

Ziggy and Maka ran over to a big mud puddle near the watering hole. "This is just the thing!" said Ziggy.

Ziggy pounced right into the middle of the puddle. Then he rolled around in the soft, squishy mud.

"Be sure to get good and muddy!" Maka shouted as he climbed up the tree. "We want to cover up each and every one of those pesky stripes!"

Ziggy squirmed and wiggled around in the mud. Before long, every last one of his stripes was covered in the thick, brown mud.

Just then, Ziggy's mother came to the watering hole and saw Ziggy rolling in the mud. She nudged him over to the water and scrubbed all the mud off of his coat.

"But, Mama," Ziggy complained, "I don't want to be striped anymore. Don't you ever get tired of being striped?"

"When I was your age, I didn't want to be striped, either," his mother said. "But then I learned that my coat is very special. Your coat is special, too."

"I guess so," sighed Ziggy as he hung his head.

Then Ziggy's mother had an idea. "Let's play a game," she said as they walked toward the jungle. "Close your eyes and count to ten, and then try to find me."

"All right, Mother," sighed Ziggy.

Ziggy had played hide-and-seek before, and he didn't see what it had to do with his stripes. But Ziggy counted anyway.

Ziggy looked around for his mother. He looked in the tall grasses. He looked behind a tree and a bush. But she was nowhere to be found.

"Mother, where are you?" called Ziggy.

"Why, I'm right here, Ziggy," said his mother, stepping out from the tall grasses right in front of him.

"But I didn't see you there at all!" exclaimed Ziggy.

"That's why our stripes are so special. Our orange stripes blend in with the grasses, and our black stripes blend in with the shadows. They make it easy for us to hide," his mother smiled.

"I guess these old stripes are not so bad after all!" giggled Ziggy. "I'm going to play with Kiko and Maka." He could hardly wait to show his friends his new trick.

Little Witch

Illustrated by Leanne Mebust

Written by Brian Conway

Little Wanda Witch kept busy studying her big book of magic spells. But she really wanted to play the day away like the other witches did.

Wanda also wanted the other witches to like her. They were older than she was, but they were the only witches to play with. Wanda thought that if she learned all of her witch's spells, she could be more like them. Magic spells are never easy, even for a smart little witch like Wanda.

"Abracadabble! That's not it," Wanda said. "Abracabubble! That's not right, either."

Sometimes the spells made Wanda dizzy. The book was full of all sorts of tricky tongue-twisting talk. But she was not the kind of witch who gave up easily. Wanda knew she could learn every last trick in that big book of spells.

"Someday," Wanda thought to herself, "I'll be big enough to boil and bubble and all that stuff."

Then Wanda was ready for her first witch's trick. She had practiced it over and over again in her mind. Now Wanda would do it for real! She hopped on one foot and twiddled her fingers, just like her big book of magic spells said. Then she pointed at her broom and chanted,

> *Broom, broom, who needs you?*
> *Warty, haggy witches do.*
> *You can sweep the floors inside.*
> *A tricycle's the thing to ride!*

Wanda felt some magic stirring in the air. It was swirling around her hands, and it kind of tickled! She pointed again, passing a zap from her hands to the broom.

POOF! It worked. Well, sort of. The broom changed, but not like Wanda wanted it to.

"Oops!" Wanda said. "That's not a tricycle. It's an icicle!"

Wanda went back to her book of spells to study some more. "I wonder what went wrong?" Wanda said to her kitten.

Wanda looked at her book. "I did everything right. It's the spell that must be wrong." So Wanda found another spell she could try right away.

"I need your help, Kitty," Wanda called. Kitty tried to hide under the table. Kitty liked being a kitty. She didn't want to turn into an icicle or a spider or a dog.

"Don't worry, Kitty," Wanda assured her. "It's an easy one. Now just stay still."

Wanda read right from the book this time. In her best witch's voice, she shrieked,

> *Abracablue and abracablots!*
> *Wouldn't Kitty be pretty*
> *With polka-dot spots?*

POOF! This trick worked, too, but not like Wanda wanted it to. Wanda got lots of spots, it's true, but they weren't on her kitten. They were on the polka-dotted puppy dogs all over her room!

Wanda buried her head in her book and wondered,
"So many puppies. What will the other witches think?"

Wanda had some troubles, but she would never give up.
She shooed the puppies out to some polka-dotted doghouses
in the yard and found a toad.

This toad didn't have a single wart on its entire body.
Wanda felt sorry for the little guy. She knew she had a spell
to get his skin as lumpy as it should be.

Wanda clicked her heels, pointed at the toad, and chanted her spell:

> *Dimples and pimples*
> *And bumps of all sorts,*
> *A toad's needs are simple:*
> *Clumps of big warts.*

POOF! Wanda's magic gently zapped the toad. When she saw what happened next, Wanda could not believe her eyes!

Could it be true? Yes! Wanda did it! Her spell worked. Wanda hurried out to the cauldron to show the other young witches her happy little toad.

"I did it! I did it!" Wanda called to the other witches. "It's my first real witch's trick. Look at how lumpy he is now."

"Oooh, what marvelous warts," the other witches cooed. "We must have some."

So Wanda tried her wonderful wart trick on the other witches. She knew what worked the first time, so she didn't change a thing.

POOF! The spell worked again! The other witches had lots of lumpy warts. But they weren't witches anymore. They were toads!

"Uh-oh," Wanda sighed.

Wanda speedily flipped through her big book of magic spells. But she couldn't find the right one to turn them back into witches.

Then Kitty brought Wanda her little witch's broom. Wanda finally remembered the first rule of witchery! It wasn't in any book. Wanda learned it from her mother when she was just a baby.

Now her mother's words came back to Wanda:

If you find you're in a mess,
Your little witch's broom's the best
For fixing messes clean and clear.
Just wave your broom around, my dear!

Wanda did just that. POOF! The warty toads became warty witches again. And they weren't mad at her at all. In fact, they thought Wanda was the smartest little witch around.

Gingerbread Man

Illustrated by Priscilla Burris

Adapted by Lisa Harkrader

145

Once upon a time Yellow Hen baked a gingerbread man. She gave him raisin eyes and a frosting nose and a wide frosting mouth.

"All done," said Yellow Hen as she added frosting buttons to his fine frosting coat. "You look delicious!"

Yellow Hen placed the Gingerbread Man on a rack to cool. But as soon as he was cooled, he jumped off the rack. Then the Gingerbread Man ran from the house.

Yellow Hen chased the Gingerbread Man out the door and

down the lane. She ran as fast as her legs would take her. But the Gingerbread Man ran even faster.

"Run, run, as fast as you can. You can't catch me. I'm the Gingerbread Man," he sang.

Soon the Gingerbread Man passed a cow chewing grass. Cow had never seen a gingerbread man running down the lane before. And she had never seen anyone running so fast.

"Yoo-hoo!" Cow called to him. "Where are you going in such a hurry?"

The Gingerbread Man didn't stop. And he didn't slow down.

"Dear me!" mooed Cow. "That gingerbread man looks better to eat than this grass. I am going to catch him."

Cow trotted off down the lane behind the Gingerbread Man. She ran as fast as her legs would take her. But the Gingerbread Man ran even faster.

"Run, run, as fast as you can. You can't catch me. I'm the Gingerbread Man," he sang.

Soon the Gingerbread Man passed a horse chomping hay. Horse had never seen a gingerbread man running down the lane before. And he had never seen anyone running so fast.

"Hello!" Horse called out. "Where are you going in such a big hurry?"

The Gingerbread Man didn't stop. And he didn't slow down.

"Well," brayed Horse, "he looks better to eat than this hay. I am going to catch him."

Horse galloped down the lane after the Gingerbread Man. He ran as fast as his legs would take him. But the Gingerbread Man ran even faster.

"Run, run, as fast as you can. You can't catch me. I'm the Gingerbread Man," he sang.

Soon the Gingerbread Man passed a pig rolling in mud. Pig had never seen a gingerbread man running down the lane before. And he had never seen anyone running so fast.

"Howdy!" Pig called out. "Where are you going in such a big hurry?"

The Gingerbread Man didn't stop. And he didn't slow down.

"Golly!" oinked Pig. "He looks better to eat than my slop. I am going to catch him."

Pig scurried down the lane after the Gingerbread Man. He ran as fast as his legs would take him. But the Gingerbread Man ran even faster.

"Run, run, as fast as you can. You can't catch me. I'm the Gingerbread Man," he sang.

Pig was pretty hungry, though. When he thought about how good the Gingerbread Man would taste, he began picking up speed. Pig wasn't about to let him get away.

Pig began to catch up to the fast cookie. He was right behind the Gingerbread Man, until he started to huff and puff.

The Gingerbread Man got away and ran to the bank of a river. He couldn't go across the river. He couldn't go around the river. And he couldn't go back down the lane where Pig, Horse, Cow, and Yellow Hen were waiting to catch him.

A sly fox lived nearby. He had never seen such a sweet gingerbread man with raisin eyes, a frosting nose, and a wide frosting mouth standing on the bank of the river before.

"Hello there, Mr. Gingerbread," Fox called out. "It seems to me you could use some help. I'd be glad to row you across the river in my boat."

Fox reached into his boat and brought out a serving tray with a lid. He lifted the lid.

"Jump in here where you'll stay dry," Fox told the Gingerbread Man. Fox licked his lips. "I'd hate for your frosting to get soggy."

The Gingerbread Man climbed onto the serving tray. Fox quickly clamped the lid down. He pushed the boat away from the shore and rowed until he reached the middle of the river. Then Fox stopped rowing and lifted the lid of the tray.

The Gingerbread Man stepped off of the tray. He saw Yellow Hen, Cow, Horse, and Pig on the shore, and waved. "They'll never be able to catch me out here," he chuckled.

"That's right, my sweet little friend," said Fox. "I'll make sure of it."

With that, Fox popped the Gingerbread Man into his mouth and, with a smack and a gulp, the Gingerbread Man was gone. He was delicious, just as Yellow Hen had said.

Bugville Bridge

Illustrated by Richard Bernal

Written by Brian Conway

Long ago, a few brave insects from the town of Bugville flew to a distant land they called Harvest Hill. There they found great giant helpings of the finest flavored foods!

There was enough food in Harvest Hill to keep all the bugs in Bugville full for many, many years! And there was nothing stopping the insects from carrying a few tasty morsels, bit by bit, back to Bugville.

The bugs had so much food that they decided to build a long bridge out of the leftovers. That way, the crawling bugs could get to Harvest Hill, too.

The insects built their special bridge in a hurry. Before long they were making the trip to Harvest Hill every day.

The bugs brought back loads of yummy treats, and everyone in Bugville was happy for a great long while.

Bugville became the jolliest place around. The bugs had Banana Festivals every Tuesday, and Chocolate Carnivals three times a week. Every bug in Bugville ate ten meals a day, and many of them took naps in between meals.

Soon the worker bees were the only ones who made the long journey to Harvest Hill. The plump little bees would cross Bugville Bridge each day and bring back enough food for everybody. But then the worker bees got lazy, too.

"I'm hungry," Benny Bee said one day as they crossed the bridge. "Let's stop for a snack."

Benny and Bessy Bee nibbled on the licorice that held the bridge together. "There's plenty of food in our bridge," Benny said. "Let's bring back some cheese, too."

Just then, Gus Grasshopper walked by. "This might be a problem," Gus said to himself.

Gus was right! The other bugs soon found out the bridge was a good place to have a snack, too. They took a little nibble here and a little munch there, but no one thought to put any food back into the bridge. Before too long the bridge crumbled down!

Lady Bug, the Queen of Bugville, called for Gus. His great-great-grandfather had helped to build Bugville Bridge so many years ago.

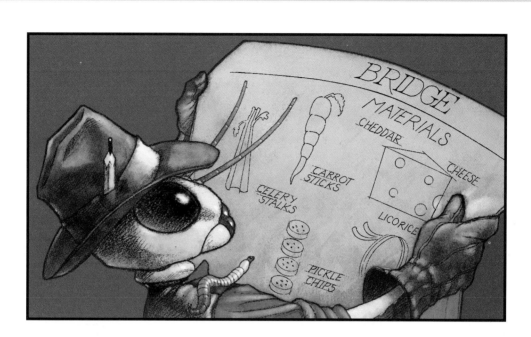

Lady Bug brought out the old plans and handed them over to him. "You'll lead the crew to build a new bridge to Harvest Hill," she told Gus. "All of Bugville is counting on you."

"We'll need carrots and celery and pretzels and cheese," Gus said. "Bugville Bridge will be better than ever if we all lend a hand!"

With Lady Bug's help, Gus Grasshopper spread the word around town. Everyone would help build the new bridge.

Every bug in Bugville had a job to do. The beetles and the caterpillars spent the whole day digging while the dragonflies brought the longest, crispiest celery stalks back from Harvest Hill.

Lady Bug was very pleased. She had never seen so much activity in Bugville.

"I just saw Daddy Longlegs get up from his rocker for the first time in ages!" she giggled to Gus.

What's more, Lady Bug was pleasantly surprised to see all the insects working together. "The mosquitos are getting along with the moths," she told Gus, "and the termites are helping the earwigs!"

A little later Gus Grasshopper asked the locusts to sound the lunch bell. He told everyone to take a break, but the busy bugs were too excited to stop.

"We'll eat later," the busy bugs said. "All of Bugville's counting on us!"

The butterflies, who usually just flew from flower to flower, asked what they could do. "We need your big wings and gentle touch to carry our carrots," Gus said.

"We won't let you down," the butterflies promised.

After only a few days, the new Bugville Bridge was coming along splendidly. The bumblebees knew where to find the sweetest red licorice and chocolate-covered pretzels in Harvest Hill.

The centipedes all got together to carry the licorice and pretzels back. They chugged along swiftly in line like an express train headed for Bugville.

The ants were in charge of the pickle chips. They found the picnic grounds in Harvest Hill without a problem, and no one had to tell the ants how to get a whole lot of food from one place to another.

At last the new Bugville Bridge was finished.

"Hurrah!" the bugs of Bugville buzzed.

Gus Grasshopper and Lady Bug beamed with pride, too.

"The bridge looks great!" cheered Gus Grasshopper.

"It looks good enough to eat," Lady Bug joked, but they all knew better than that.

This new bridge really was better than the last one. It was tall and strong and built to last. And best of all, the bugs of Bugville did it together.

Birthday Cake Mix-Up

Illustrated by Sherry Neidigh

Written by Sarah Toast

Adapted by Lisa Harkrader

Barry Bumblebee sat straight up in bed. He rubbed his eyes and looked out the window.

"Oh, no!" cried Barry. "The sun is up. I'm late."

Barry had to go to work before most bugs in town were even awake. He was the owner of the Busy Bee Bakery. The bakery made the most delicious baked goods in town.

Barry pulled on his white apron and baker's hat. Then he rushed out the door.

When Barry arrived at the bakery, his helpers were already busy. Two bees sifted flour, while another bee measured cinnamon for a batch of sticky buns. Three other bees mixed batter for the blueberry muffins.

"The muffins will be done soon," the bees told Barry. "We have cherry popovers in the oven, and pumpernickel rolls cooling on a rack. The only things left to make are raisin bread and chocolate chip cookies."

"I'll take care of the rest," said Barry.

He reached in his pocket for his glasses. But they weren't there. "Oh, no!" cried Barry. "Now where did I leave my glasses?"

Barry squinted at the clock. The bakery would be opening soon. There was no time to look for his glasses!

"I bake raisin bread and chocolate chip cookies every day," said Barry. "I don't need my glasses."

Barry set out two mixing bowls. He measured flour, sugar, and butter for the cookies with one hand, and mixed bread batter with another.

"I can't forget the main ingredients," said Barry.

He pulled a box of raisins and a bag of chocolate chips from the cupboard. Barry poured the raisins into one bowl and the chocolate chips into the other. He mixed both batters. Then Barry finished making the cookies and the bread, and put them into the oven.

Soon the oven timer dinged. Barry squinted at the clock.

"Time to take my goodies from the oven and open the Busy Bee Bakery," he said.

Barry set the cookies and bread on a tray. Just then his first two customers arrived, Carla and Casey Cricket. "Good morning, Barry!"

"You're just in time to taste some freshly baked treats," he said. Barry gave Carla a slice of bread and handed Casey a cookie.

"I love raisin cookies," said Casey.

"Mmm," said Carla. "I've never tasted chocolate chip bread before."

"Chocolate chip bread?" said Barry. "Raisin cookies? Oh, no! I mixed up the ingredients. I'll have to start all over."

"Don't do that," said Carla as she gulped down the last bite of her bread. "I have an idea."

Carla made two signs. For the cookies she wrote, "Barry's Special Recipe Raisin Cookies." For the chocolate chip bread she wrote, "A Treat You Won't Find in Any Other Bakery."

"Thank you," said Barry. "Now I need to bake a birthday cake for my niece Bibi."

Barry pulled out his cookbook. He squinted at Bibi's favorite cake recipe.

"A crate of flour," he read. "A whole crate? That seems like an awful lot. But that's what the recipe calls for." Barry dumped a crate of flour into his biggest mixing bowl.

"Two dozen eggs," Barry read. "If that's what it says, that's what I'll do."

Barry cracked two dozen eggs, and mixed them into the flour. He added a can of baking powder, a sack of sugar, and ten bags of chocolate drops. He poured the batter into his biggest cake pan, and set it in the oven.

When the timer dinged, Barry peeked into the oven.

"Oh, no!" he cried. "This cake is huge!"

The other bees helped him pull the cake from the oven. It was the biggest cake any of them had ever seen.

"I wanted to make Bibi something wonderful and ended up making something terrible," moaned Barry. "I should've used two eggs, not two dozen. And a cup of flour, not a crate."

Barry squinted at the clock again. "I don't have time to bake another one," he said.

The bees frosted the cake, and set it on a cart. "It's not so bad," they told him.

But Barry didn't believe them. He rolled the giant cake to Bibi's house anyway.

"I hope Bibi isn't too disappointed," he said to himself.

The party had already started. The guests took one look at the cake and gasped.

Barry shook his head. "Bibi, I'm sorry."

"For what?" Bibi threw her arms around her uncle, and gave him a hug. "This is the most wonderful birthday cake I've ever seen. Nobody else has ever had a cake so big. Uncle Barry, you're the greatest."

The other guests began to clap. Barry sighed with relief.

At the end of the party Bibi gave her uncle a surprise. "I found your glasses," she said. "I hope you didn't need them at work today."

Baby Bluebird

Illustrated by Cristina Ong

Written by Lisa Harkrader

Baby Bluebird looked up at the sky. She watched all the other birds flying. "It's spring," she said. "I should be flying also, but I don't know how to start." Her friend Rabbit watched the birds, too.

"Flying looks a lot like hopping," said Rabbit. "In fact, I see birds hopping about all the time. Practice hopping with me. If you hop high enough, you might start to fly."

Rabbit hopped off through the garden. Baby Bluebird hopped after her. She was in the air, but soon came back down to the ground. Baby Bluebird tried again and again.

"What do you think, Baby Bluebird?" asked Rabbit. "Is hopping like flying?"

"It's a little like flying," she said. "But I keep landing. I don't think real flying is so bouncy."

Baby Bluebird sat down in the pasture. She watched the other birds as they hopped and lifted off the ground.

Her friend Gopher watched the birds, too.

"It seems to me," said Gopher, "that flying is a lot like digging. Maybe if you practice digging with me, it will help you learn to flap your wings and fly. And digging is so much fun!"

Gopher popped down into his hole. Then he began digging through the pasture.

"It doesn't look like much fun to me," said Baby Bluebird, "but I'll give it a try."

Baby Bluebird found a nice big patch of dirt. She flapped her wings on the ground, trying to dig a hole. But the dirt was too hard, and her feathers were too soft.

All her flapping didn't help Baby Bluebird fly, but it did raise a huge cloud of dust. Baby Bluebird coughed and sneezed and wheezed.

"Maybe digging isn't like flying after all," she said. "I don't think flying is so sneezy."

Baby Bluebird fluttered her wings to get the dust out of her feathers. She sat down in the grass and looked at the birds taking off.

The birds hopped off the ground, then quickly flapped their wings. They flew as if the breezes gently carried them through the air.

"What is their secret?" Baby Bluebird wondered as the birds flew over her. "I can hop. I can flap my wings. But I still can't fly."

Her friend Turtle watched the birds, too.

"Flying looks a little like swimming," he said. "Maybe if you practice swimming through the water with me, it will help you learn to glide through the air when you fly."

Baby Bluebird watched Turtle glide around the farm pond. "That doesn't look so hard," she said.

She plunged into the water. "Oh, my! It's so wet!" she cried.

"Paddle out here to the middle," said Turtle.

Baby Bluebird tried to paddle. She splashed and sputtered and glugged. Baby Bluebird wanted to glide like Turtle. But she couldn't.

"Maybe swimming isn't like flying after all," she said. "I don't think flying is so soggy."

Baby Bluebird pulled herself on to the grassy edge of the pond. She fluttered her wings to dry them.

When her wings were dry, Baby Bluebird went to the farmhouse and found Cat and Dog curled up on the porch. Baby Bluebird sat down beside them and watched the birds flying above her.

The birds playfully swooped through the sky. As they flew, they even sang a pretty song.

"These birds can fly *and* sing," said Baby Bluebird.

Cat and Dog watched and heard the birds, too.

"They look happy," said Cat.

"We sing when we're happy," said Dog.

"Maybe singing is part of flying," said Cat. "If you sing loud enough and long enough, maybe you'll begin to fly, too. We'll help you."

Dog howled. Cat yowled. Baby Bluebird tweeted. Then she twittered. She cheeped and chirped. She took a deep breath and let out a squawk! But nobody started to fly. Not Dog. Not Cat. Not Baby Bluebird.

"It's no use," said Baby Bluebird. "Singing won't make me fly. I might as well stop trying."

"Thank goodness," said Dog. "I don't have any howls left."

"Stop trying?" said Cat. "You can't stop trying. If you want to fly, you must find a way."

Baby Bluebird sat down on the porch steps and put her head in her wings. Suddenly, she looked up.

"Singing wasn't enough. And neither was hopping or flapping or gliding," she said. "But I think I know what I need to do."

Baby Bluebird took a running start. She hopped like Rabbit. She flapped her wings like Gopher. Once she was in the air, she glided like Turtle and the other birds through the beautiful sky.

"I'm flying!" she chirped.

Baby Bluebird swooped through the clouds. She flitted from tree to tree. Then Baby Bluebird lifted her head and, like Cat and Dog, began to sing.

Little Airplane

Illustrated by Steve Boswick

Written by Conor Wolf

Adapted by J. Erik Gudell

One morning at the airport, Little Airplane wanted to fly to a birthday party with his friend Helicopter. The party was on the other side of Big Mountain.

"Rocket's party will be great," Little Airplane said to Helicopter.

Little Airplane also told Helicopter about the stunt plane who was going to perform. She could fly upside down and do loop-the-loops. And they were going to play games, like air tag and hide-and-seek.

"Wow, that sounds like a lot of fun," said Helicopter. "But

the party is far from here and a storm is coming."

Little Airplane didn't seem to mind. After all, Big Mountain didn't look that far away, and what harm could a little rain cloud do?

"Who is afraid of a little cloud?" he said. "Not me."

"Yeah," Helicopter agreed. "Me, neither."

The two of them went to the runway to wait their turn for takeoff. Before they could leave, they needed to tell Control Tower. Control Tower always needs to know who lands and who takes off from the runway.

Little Airplane signaled to Control Tower on his radio. "We are ready for takeoff," he said.

"You two should not fly today," Control Tower warned. "A big rain cloud named Storm is coming our way!"

"Who's afraid of Storm?" asked Little Airplane.

"Not us!" said Little Airplane and Helicopter as they took off. They quickly flew high into the sky.

Control Tower was a bit worried. "I hope they make it alright," she said to herself. "Storm is nothing but trouble."

The two best friends flew toward Big Mountain. The sky was bright and sunny, except for some clouds. The clouds seemed far off in the distance.

"See," said Little Airplane, "it's a perfect day for flying." Helicopter looked at the blue sky and nodded.

Little Airplane and Helicopter enjoyed their trip a lot. They flew very high in the sky and traveled over beautiful rivers and forests.

Helicopter was used to flying on long trips, but Little Airplane wasn't. He started getting tired.

"I didn't think Rocket's party was so far away," said Little Airplane. "I guess we should have asked Control Tower how long it would take us to get there."

"We're also getting very close to those clouds," said Helicopter.

"Who is afraid of a cloud?" asked Little Airplane. "Not me!"

Helicopter didn't say anything. He wasn't feeling so sure anymore.

They flew for a bit longer. But Little Airplane's tired little motor started to make a funny clanking noise.

"I think we should stop and check out that noise," said Helicopter. "Look, there's Big Mountain up ahead. Storm will never find us there."

The two landed on the mountaintop. Helicopter checked Little Airplane's engine. "I think I know what the problem is," said Helicopter. "You need some oil."

Helicopter oiled the engine, but it was too late. Little Airplane's noisy motor woke a big cloud sleeping on the other side of the mountain. It was Storm!

"Who is there?" Storm shouted as he puffed up into a big rain cloud.

"We are," answered Little Airplane and Helicopter.

"Who is afraid of me?" asked Storm.

"We are!" said Little Airplane and Helicopter as they quickly took off.

Storm chased after them. He was right on their tails, blowing wind and rain.

"We've got to get away!" yelled Little Airplane. "Or Storm will blow us off course!"

Helicopter came up with a plan. "See those fluffy clouds up ahead? Let's hide in them."

Little Airplane and Helicopter flew toward the clouds as fast as they could. Storm tried to keep up.

When they got to the fluffy clouds, Little Airplane and Helicopter dove in and hid. Storm blew so much wind and rain that he could not see where Little Airplane and Helicopter went. He blew right by them.

"Sneaky aircraft," grumbled Storm. "Where did they go? I can't find them anywhere."

After Storm passed, the sky was quiet once again. Little Airplane and Helicopter peeked out of the clouds.

"Where are we?" asked Helicopter.

Little Airplane didn't know. He called for help on his radio. "Come in Control Tower. This is Little Airplane and Helicopter. We are ready to come back, but we are lost."

"You'll be all right," replied Control Tower. "Follow my signal home."

Control Tower guided Little Airplane and Helicopter all the way back. When they saw the airport, they were filled with relief.

"All clear for landing," said Control Tower.

Little Airplane and Helicopter landed safely. They thanked Control Tower for her help.

"We missed Rocket's big party, but at least we are safe," said Helicopter.

Little Airplane agreed. "Who is happy to be home?"

"We are," Little Airplane and Helicopter said.

"Who is afraid of a big cloud?" asked Little Airplane.

"WE ARE!" they both shouted.

Elly's Little Friend

Illustrated by Debbie Pinkney

Written by Catherine McCafferty

Adapted by Lisa Harkrader

Elly thundered through the grass to where her mother was grazing. "Mama! Mama!" she called out, "I've made a new friend!"

Elly was proud of her news. She was the youngest elephant in her family, and she didn't do things by herself very often.

Elly's mother nuzzled Elly with her trunk.

"I knew you could make friends if you tried," she said. "Tell me all about this new pal of yours."

"Her name is Mindy," said Elly. "She's smart and she's funny. We met under the big, shady tree. That's my favorite spot to play, and it's Mindy's favorite spot, too. As soon as we started talking, we knew we would be friends."

"Well, it sounds like you and Mindy are a lot alike," said Elly's mother.

"We are!" said Elly.

"Why don't you invite Mindy for dinner?" said her mother. "Then our whole family can meet her."

"Hooray!" cheered Elly.

Elly was so happy she raised her trunk and let out a loud trumpeting sound. She ran back to the big, shady tree to tell Mindy the good news.

"You'll like eating dinner with us," Elly told her friend. "My family gathers the most tender leaves. I'll make sure yours are torn up very small so you can eat them. My mother and my sisters can't wait to meet you."

"I hope they like me," said Mindy.

"They'll love you," said Elly.

Mindy scrambled up onto Elly's trunk. Then the two friends went to meet Elly's family for dinner.

Elly's mother and sisters didn't see Mindy at first. "Mama," Elly said as she lifted her trunk, "this is Mindy."

"A mouse!" shouted Elly's sister. Elly's family stomped, thundered, and trumpeted away from Elly and her friend.

Mindy watched Elly's family leave. "They didn't like me at all," she squeaked softly.

Elly smiled. "They barely met you," she said. "Once they know you, I'm sure they'll like you as much as I do."

"Maybe you should come to my house instead," said Mindy. "My family should be eating dinner now. Do you like nuts?"

"I love nuts," said Elly.

Mindy and Elly set out over the grass. Mindy again rode on Elly's trunk. But it was worse at Mindy's house. Her family heard Elly's heavy footsteps coming and scampered away before Elly could say hello.

"Your family doesn't like me, either," said Elly.

"How can they not like you?" said Mindy. "They didn't even meet you. I don't understand." Mindy shook her tiny head sadly. "If they'd talk to you, they'd like you as much as I do."

Elly's eyes brightened. "That's it, Mindy! I'll tell my mama and my sisters to just talk to you. Once they talk to you, they'll love you."

"I'll tell my family the same thing," said Mindy.

As Mindy left to tell her family, Elly went to talk to her mother and sisters. She found them by the watering hole.

"Mama, if you'd just give Mindy a chance," said Elly. "You'd like her. I know you would."

"I'm sorry, Elly," said her mother, "but elephants have never liked mice."

"They dart around," said Elly's sister.

"And they squeak!" added her other sister.

Elly trudged back to the big, shady tree, her trunk hanging low. Mindy was already there.

"It's no use," said Mindy. "My family is afraid of you. They think you'll trample us."

"I wouldn't," said Elly.

"I know," said Mindy, "and I would never hurt your family."

"Elephants and mice are a lot alike," said Elly. "We both have lovely big ears."

Elly picked up a stick and drew a picture of an elephant on the ground. Then Mindy picked up a stick, too. She drew a

picture of a mouse in front of her.

"We both have four legs and long, skinny tails," Elly sniffed back a tear. "Why can't our families see that?"

Mindy gulped. "Maybe we shouldn't be friends."

"But I'd miss you," Elly said sadly. Her big tears turned the dust to mud.

Elly's mother saw Elly crying from the watering hole. She ran up to dry off her daughter's tears with a large leaf.

Mindy's mother saw Mindy crying from behind a tree. She ran up to wipe Mindy's face with a tiny leaf.

The two mothers stopped to look at each other. "Maybe our families are alike after all," said Elly's mother.

Mindy's mother pointed to the drawings. "Maybe we are."

"Elly and Mindy would be sad if we separated them," said Elly's mother.

Mindy's mother nodded. "We couldn't do that to them. We should try to get along."

Elly's mother agreed. Soon Mindy's family got an elephant's-eye view of the world. And Elly's family learned to enjoy the little things in life.

Puppy Tale

Illustrated by Kathy Wilburn

Written by Catherine McCafferty

Adapted by Brian Conway

Sparky lived on a farm in the country. He was as curious and as busy as a farm puppy could be. Sparky searched and sniffed his way around every inch of that big farm.

One day Sparky's father asked him, "Son, what in the world are you looking for?"

"I smell something that smells like fun," Sparky answered. "I don't know what it is, but I'll know when I find it." And off he went.

Sparky's father chuckled. He remembered when he himself was the busiest pup in the litter. At least Sparky wasn't bothering the cows at milking time or rolling in the mud with the pigs or causing trouble in the henhouse!

A little later, on the other side of the meadow, Sparky caught a scent. And it smelled like something that smelled like fun!

In the woods at the edge of the meadow, Sparky dug through some leaves. He found a big toy bone buried there!

Sparky loved his new toy bone. It was perfect for chewing and chomping. He brought it home to show his father.

"I found it!" said Sparky. "And I was right. It's a fun toy!"

"Well, what do you know," Sparky's father said. "I haven't seen that bone in years! That was my toy bone when I was a pup your age!"

Sparky's father had lost that toy bone long ago. He had looked for it way back then, but he never caught the slightest scent of it. Then he'd forgotten all about it.

"It was buried in the woods beside the meadow," Sparky said. "Like buried treasure!"

"Son, I'm proud of you," said Sparky's father. "You are one fine finder!"

"Can I have it?" Sparky asked.

"You found it, so it's yours," his father said. "Just be sure you take care of that bone. Don't lose it like I did."

Sparky promised he'd never lose his new toy. He kept it with him all the time. Sparky even held the toy bone while he slept.

Sparky brought the bone to breakfast. And he even brought the bone to the pasture where they watched the sheep.

But Sparky didn't watch the sheep. He chomped the bone most of the time, and, when he wasn't busy chewing, he kept a watchful eye on his toy bone. He didn't want to lose it.

Sparky's brother and sister didn't like the toy bone. Sparky thought they must be jealous. He had the bone, and they didn't. So Sparky offered to share it with them.

"We don't want it," they told Sparky. "We want to play

circle-chase. But you never play with us anymore!"

Sparky said he would play with them for a little while. Every time he turned, though, Sparky bumped his brother and sister with the big toy bone.

Sparky's father said, "Son, you can't keep running around with that toy bone all the time. Someone might get hurt."

"But I don't want to lose it," said Sparky.

Sparky's father brought him out to the edge of the meadow. "Let me show you something I learned when I was a pup," he said. "We'll dig a hole that you can use to hide your bone."

Sparky and his father buried the bone in the dirt. Now no one would know where it was hidden.

"Whenever you want your bone, all you have to do is dig it up again," Sparky's father told him. "This way you don't have to carry it around all the time. And you can be sure it's in a safe place, even when it's not with you."

"This is great!" said Sparky. "Now I can leave the bone, and only I will know where it is."

"Don't forget where you buried it, Sparky," his father reminded him.

"I promise I won't forget," Sparky said.

Sparky barked happily, calling his brother and sister out to the meadow. They came to see what was going on.

"Now I can play with you again," Sparky cheered.

"What happened to your toy bone?" his sister asked.

"Yeah," said his brother, "did you lose it?"

Sparky smiled at his father. "I can't tell you where it is," Sparky said, "but if you ever want to play with it, I'll know where to find it."

Sparky jumped to chase his brother, snapping playfully at his feet. His brother chased their sister, and their sister chased Sparky.

And nobody bumped into anyone else! It was the best time they'd had together in a while.

They played circle-chase all day long. Sparky had been so busy with his new toy bone, he had forgotten what fun it was to play with his family!

Jack and the Beanstalk

Illustrated by Wendy Edelson

Adapted by Sarah Toast

Once upon a time, there lived a mouse named Jack who lived with his mother in the country. They were good, honest mice, but they were poor.

But Jack and his mother hadn't always been so poor. When Jack's father was alive, a fairy godmother repaid his kindness by giving him a magic golden cheese that grew back when it was eaten. But one day a mean giant cat stole the cheese and killed Jack's father.

Jack's mother worked hard to grow enough vegetables to feed herself and her boy. Usually there were some left over to trade for cheese.

One year there wasn't enough rain to grow a good crop of vegetables. Jack was good-natured, but he didn't work hard to help his mother find enough food to eat. His mother had to sell almost everything they had.

Finally there was nothing left in the cupboard to eat. And there was nothing left to sell but the cart.

When times were better, Jack had pulled their vegetables to town on the cart to trade them for cheese. But without the vegetables, they no longer had use for it.

"Jack, take our cart to town one last time," said his mother. "You can get a good price for it."

Jack took the cart to the storekeeper. He stroked his whiskers in thought.

"Young mouse," he said, "I'm going to reach into my bag and pick out three very special magic beans to trade for your cart."

Jack was delighted to get three magic beans for only one cart. He scampered back home to his mother.

"What did you get for the cart, dear Jack?" his mother asked warmly.

"I got three very special magic beans!" Jack told her with pride.

"You foolish boy!" cried his mother. "There's no such thing as magic beans! Now we have nothing left to sell."

Jack's mother threw the beans out the window. Then she and Jack went to bed without any supper.

The next morning Jack woke up thinking about how nice some breakfast would be. Then he opened his eyes.

Jack saw a tangle of leaves at his window. He got out of bed and took a closer look. Jack saw that a huge beanstalk had sprung up over night. It had grown taller than anything in his mother's garden and straight up through the clouds.

"I wonder where the top of the beanstalk ends?" Jack thought to himself. He climbed out his bedroom window and began to climb the tall beanstalk.

Jack climbed for hours. When he finally climbed through the clouds, he saw a wonderful castle in the distance. Even though Jack was now tired and hungry, he walked until he reached the castle.

Jack scrambled up the castle wall to an open window and peered inside. On the floor was a huge golden cheese that smelled incredibly delicious. But a giant cat guarded the cheese.

Hungry Jack had to get to that cheese! Quickly, he scampered back out on the castle wall and dashed to the next window.

Perched on the windowsill, Jack scratched and squeaked with all his might. Soon the giant came into the room to see what the noise was all about.

Jack dashed back along the outside wall to the first window, where the golden cheese stood unguarded. Jack hopped down and nibbled at the cheese. It tasted so good!

Just then Jack heard the giant complaining in the next room. "Fee, fi, fo, fouse. I smell a mouse in this old house! Come out, come out!"

Jack quickly broke off an enormous piece of cheese. He ran around the corner with it just as the giant came back to guard his golden treasure.

"I know you're around here somewhere," said the giant cat.

The giant looked all around, but he could not find Jack. The smell of the big cheese had covered up the smell of little Jack, so the giant never knew how close he had been to catching him.

"I must hurry," Jack thought to himself.

He ran across the clouds to the beanstalk. As fast as he could, Jack climbed down with the cheese.

"Mother," he called, "bring me the ax."

"Right away!" she called back.

When Jack reached the ground, he chopped down the beanstalk. And his mother danced around the piece of golden cheese.

Jack's mother told him, "This is a piece of the magic golden cheese that the giant stole from your father. Your magic beans helped us get it back!"

That evening Jack and his mother ate their fill, but they left some cheese uneaten. They put it away in the cupboard where it would grow back to its full size overnight.

"You are a good boy, Jack!" said his mother. They never went hungry again.

Rookie Fire Truck

Illustrated by Jim Talbot

Written by Tom Lynch

Adapted by Brian Conway

Rookie was a brand new fire truck. His shiny chrome horns, brand new tires, and brilliant red coat of paint made Rookie really stand out.

Rookie's ladder was clean and white, without a footprint on it, and his fire hose had never sprayed a flame. That's because Rookie had never fought a real fire before.

Rookie learned how to fight fires in fire truck school. He practiced and practiced until he got everything right. Then Rookie was ready for some real action. He was sent to work at the big firehouse in town.

Everybody in town looked up and waved when Rookie drove by. He wore a proud, happy smile for his new neighbors.

Then Rookie gave them all a soft toot of his horn and a friendly flash of his signal. He was very excited about his first day at the firehouse.

"This must be the place," he said to himself. "I can't wait to meet my new friends."

The first fire truck Rookie met that day was Big Red. He was the oldest fire truck at the station. Rookie didn't know it yet, but Big Red could also be the meanest fire truck around.

"Hello, there," Rookie said to Big Red. "I'm very glad to meet you."

"Sure you are," Big Red snarled, "but are you ready to work, Rookie?"

"I learned a lot at school," Rookie answered earnestly. "When the fire alarm sounds, I'll be ready!"

Big Red just laughed. "You think your fire drills in school got you ready to fight real fires?" he asked.

"Yes, sir!" Rookie said. "We learned to hurry to the scene. I know about keeping my tank filled with water and how to spray the fire away. We practiced search-and-rescue and fire safety, too. It was fun!"

"Well, I've got news for you, Rookie," Big Red said. "Firefighting is never fun, and it sure isn't pretty, either."

Big Red rolled away laughing. Rookie felt so bad his tires almost went flat. And the other trucks weren't very nice to Rookie, either.

"Pretty little thing," Eleanor Engine teased. "He never fought a fire before."

"Don't get your shiny, new paint dirty, kid," chuckled Larry the Ladder Truck.

Rookie was very sad and lonely. He never thought that fire trucks could be so cruel. All they saw was his shiny coat of paint and squeaky clean equipment. Rookie wondered why the other trucks had to tease him so.

Rookie stayed outside all night long. He sprayed his windshield so the other trucks wouldn't know he was crying.

"If only I could prove what a good firefighter I am," Rookie thought. "Then they might like me."

Late that night Rookie had his chance. The alarm sounded, and Rookie was ready to go! He zoomed into action before the other trucks had even left the station house. Rookie was the first fire truck on the scene!

"That alone should impress the other trucks," Rookie thought to himself. He aimed his hose at the fire.

A sudden, booming horn blow startled Rookie. It was Big Red, who bumped his way through to the building.

"Outta my way, Rookie. I'll handle this," said Big Red.

Then Larry the Ladder Truck and Eleanor Engine arrived. They all moved in front of Rookie Fire Truck. He had no room left to help them out.

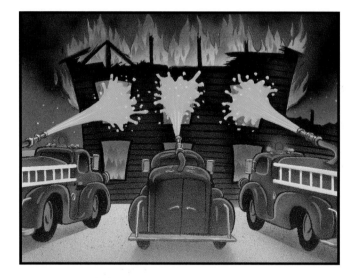

Rookie noticed the other fire trucks were awfully close to the burning building. In school, Rookie had learned to keep his distance from the flames. That's because all the fire safety books had said, "Let the water get close for you."

Rookie tried to warn the others. "Please pull back," he called. "This building could tumble down upon you!"

The older trucks were too busy to listen. They just sounded their sirens more loudly and ignored him.

Rookie Fire Truck could only watch. It was a good thing someone was watching carefully, though, because something terrible happened next. Big Red ran out of water!

The fire rippled over the ground, spreading more quickly than any fire truck could move. The flames surrounded Big Red until he could not escape.

"I've got you covered," said Rookie.

Rookie rushed over to help at once. As the flames grazed Big Red's tires, Rookie soaked the ground around Big Red. Then he fought the fire back, back, back until all the flames were gone.

There among clouds of dark smoke, the older trucks rolled through the ashes to the spot where Rookie was. "I guess we need someone younger on our team to watch our backs," Larry the Ladder Truck said.

"Hey, kid," Eleanor Engine nudged him, "those sooty spots kinda make you look older."

"You did good," said Big Red kindly. The gruff old fire truck even smiled when he said, "You're one of us now, Rookie."

Grasshopper Grocery

Illustrated by Mary Lou Faltico

Written by Sarah Toast

Adapted by Brian Conway

Gilbert and Goldie Grasshopper got to their grocery store early every morning. They had to be there before the delivery truck arrived.

"Good morning, Benny," Gilbert Grasshopper greeted the delivery driver, as he did every morning. "Is the fruit nice and fresh today?"

"Any fresher, they'd still be seeds," Benny answered, as he did every morning. And every morning, that brought a smile to their faces.

All the food in the store had to be fresh every day. The Fruit Flies were especially picky about the apples and oranges, but Gilbert and Goldie's goods never disappointed them.

Gilbert and Goldie had the best food in town. That's why all the bugs shopped at the Grasshopper Grocery.

Gilbert and Goldie stocked the store for the morning rush. They put all the food where it needed to go. Vegetables and fruit went out front. Ice cream went in the freezer, and cans went on the shelves.

Gilbert and Goldie were ready for another busy day at their little store.

"The Grasshopper Grocery is open for business!" Goldie told Gilbert.

Lily and Lampert Locust were the first to arrive that morning. They brought all the little Locusts with them.

Goldie knew how very busy these little bugs could be. Gilbert and Goldie needed to keep an eye on them.

"I'll get it, Lisa," Lloyd said, reaching for the top apple. Lisa thought the whole pile would topple down.

Goldie thought so, too, but Lloyd hopped up. Then he flapped his wings until he reached it.

Meanwhile, little Lucas Locust, the baby boy of the family, picked up all his favorite goodies. Lucas would eat anything. It didn't matter what it was. He liked blue things and green things the best. Lily told Lucas he could have the green watermelon, but the blue juice and the cookies would have to go back on the shelf.

Mr. Lambert Locust picked up the cookies, though. He slipped them into his own grocery basket.

Now every bug knows that Locusts love fruit as much as Fruit Flies do. They'd eat it straight out of the orchard if they could, so Goldie Grasshopper helped Lambert and Lily choose fruit.

"Toss me an orange," Lambert called to Goldie. "I'm open."

Lily Locust giggled. Sometimes she wondered who had more fun at the store, Lambert or the children.

Goldie could toss many fruits at once. "Here's a good one, Lambert," she said.

On the other side of the store, Gilbert Grasshopper helped the little Locusts. They knew how to make shopping fun. It wasn't so much fun for Gilbert, though.

"Look out, Lisa!" he cried. "You're holding too many things at once!" Gilbert didn't want to see his nice groceries tumble down to the floor.

"No flying in the store, please," he said with a sigh. "And, remember, kids, shopping carts are not made for racing!"

"Weeeee!" shrieked little Lucas Locust.

The Locust family had everything they needed and more! Lily Locust said, "Let's put back all the extra things now."

Lambert and the children agreed to put the bubble gum, the sour candies, and the three extra bags of potato chips back on the shelves.

"Lambert!" Lily called to her husband. "These cookies go back, too."

The little Locusts loved to help at the checkout counter. That's because it moved!

Lloyd liked to slide along the rolling counter like an airplane getting ready for takeoff.

Little Lucas tried it once and ended up in a paper sack. He never tried that again.

Goldie Grasshopper added up the bill. Lily paid for all the goodies at the cash register. Goldie wondered how one family could eat so much in a week!

"I still think we need more potato chips," Lisa Locust said.

"But we'll be back tomorrow, Lisa," said Lily. "This food is just for today."

After the busy Locust family left, Gilbert and Goldie needed a break.

"The store is all out of order now," Gilbert said. "The pears are with the pretzels, the soup's in the freezer, and the soda pop is with the celery!"

"Let's go to lunch, Gilbert," Goldie said. "We can set up all over again when we get back."

Gilbert and Goldie Grasshopper decided to go on a picnic in Butterfly Park. Goldie closed up the shop, and Gilbert carried out the biggest watermelon they got from their delivery that day.

Gilbert always set aside the finest fruit just for them. This was the best thing about being the owners of the Grasshopper Grocery. The Locusts might make a mess, and the Fireflies might stay too late, but the greatest tasty goodies made it all worthwhile.

"Yum!" said Gilbert. "There's no better treat than cold watermelon in the middle of a hot day."

Gilbert and Goldie were glad to be grocers.

Good Morning Farm

Illustrated by Lee Duggan

Written by Sarah Toast

Adapted by David Presser

Every morning Rooster happily greeted the sun with a big, "Cock-a-doodle-doo!" But on this morning, he was especially excited. Rooster scratched his claws on the ground. He couldn't wait to crow.

Rooster hopped up onto the fence, puffed out his chest, and spread his wings. Then he let out an even bigger and louder crow than usual.

"Cock-a-doodle-doo! Cock-a-doodle-doo!" he crowed. "Cock-a-doodle-doo-doo-doo!"

"My, my, that's a special greeting this morning," said the bright sun. "It's good to see you so happy."

Rooster hopped up and down on the fence. Then he puffed himself up and said to the sun, "I have a surprise this morning that I cannot wait to show the other animals!"

"Well, you'd better go wake them up then," said the sun.

Rooster agreed and flew off. He flew as fast as he could over to the pig pen.

When he got there, Rooster found Pig sleeping. He flapped his wings loudly and crowed, "Cock-a-doodle-doo-doo-doo!" But Pig didn't wake up.

"Wake up!" said Rooster. "I have a big surprise! Come with me and see!"

"I am surprised you woke me up," Pig said with a startled oink. "But I will come with you and see this big surprise of yours, just as soon as I am ready."

Rooster walked back and forth waiting for Pig. Pig slowly yawned and stretched. Then he rolled in the mud, not once, but twice. Pig was ready now.

Rooster and Pig hurried over to the barn. They found Cow sleeping in her bed of straw.

Rooster gently landed on top of Cow's head and crowed, "Cock-a-doodle-doo-doo-doo!"

"Good Morning, Rooster. Good Morning, Pig," mooed Cow.

"I have a big surprise to show you," said Rooster.

"How exciting! I can't wait to see it," said Cow as she shook off some straw. "Let's get moving!"

Rooster, Pig, and Cow went out to the pasture to find Lamb. She was sleeping by some flowers.

"Cock-a-doodle-doo-doo-doo! I've got a big surprise this morning," said Rooster.

"Rooster, this must be a good surprise. You seem very excited," said Lamb as she wiped her eyes. "I wonder what it could be?"

"Cow and I would like to know, too," said Pig. "Why don't we all go together and see!"

"Come with me!" said Rooster.

Rooster flew up into the sky ahead of his friends to lead the way. Pig, Cow, and Lamb followed.

"Where are we going?" asked Lamb.

"Are we almost there?" asked Pig. "I'm hungry."

"Me, too," said Cow.

"You'll just have to wait," said Rooster.

As they walked on, Pig, Cow, and Lamb tried to guess what the big surprise could be. What was Rooster so excited about? What special thing were they about to see?

"Maybe it's a new trough," oinked Pig.

Pig had a wonderful picture in his head. He saw himself eating out of a huge trough filled with delicous food.

There would be lots of corn and bread, which were his favorites. Then he saw himself having a dessert of tasty apples.

Cow had a different idea. "Maybe it's a new pasture," said Cow.

Cow also had a wonderful picture in her head. She saw herself eating in a huge field of sweet clover. Then she saw herself taking a nice nap on the soft grass.

Lamb thought that Cow and Pig had some good guesses. But she didn't think Rooster would be excited about a new trough or pasture.

"I can't guess what it could be," she said.

Pig, Cow, and Lamb followed Rooster all the way to the other side of the farm. They finally stopped when Rooster perched on the wooden fence outside of the hen house.

Rooster turned to the other animals. "You're probably wondering why I called you all here," he said.

"Yes, we are," oinked Pig.

"Tell us more," mooed Cow.

"I can barely stand waiting," bleated Lamb.

"Well, look over there," crowed Rooster. He walked across the yard over to the hen house.

The animals heard a strange sound. It was a peeping sound. What could it be? Then the animals looked over by the hay and saw what made those noisy sounds.

There were six newly hatched baby chicks! They were taking their first breaths and waving their little wings. They looked up at Mama Hen and Rooster, then chirped.

Rooster was a proud papa. He puffed himself all up and flapped his wings.

"What a great surprise!" said Pig, Cow, and Lamb. They all listened to the cheerful little chicks cheep and chirp. One chick even said a cock-a-doodle-doo, just like his papa.

Tiny Ghost

Illustrated by Leanne Mebust

Written by Brian Conway

That new house was too much for Tiny. Sure, it was a good house for haunting. It was cold and damp and drafty. It had creepy cobwebs in every corner, creaky cracks in the floors, and several shutters that shook. The big spooky house even had lots of people to scare.

"Boo!" shouted Tiny Ghost, just as loud as he could.

"Did you hear something?" a nice lady asked. "Something like a mouse?"

Tiny took a deep breath. He let out a big "BOOGALOOGA!"

"Please pass the salt," a large man said.

Who'd be afraid of a little, tiny ghost creeping around a big, old house?

Nobody there was scared of Tiny. He was no bigger than a salt shaker! That was the biggest problem for Tiny Ghost.

Even when people saw him, they'd just say he was a cute little fellow. That had happened at Tiny's last house.

So no one noticed when Tiny left to find a better house.

Tiny looked through town all morning. All the houses were made for bigger ghosts.

As Tiny flew through a yard, he heard a growling sound. Tiny liked scary sounds. They made him feel at home.

When he got closer, he found out the noise was coming from a little house in the yard. Finally he found a small house to haunt! It was damp and dark, like the last one. And it was a bit smelly, too!

"How wonderful!" Tiny said to himself. "Yes, this might be the right house for me!"

Of course, it couldn't be Tiny's haunted house unless Tiny could scare whoever lived there.

"Let's see if this dog is a scaredy cat!" Tiny said.

Tiny waved his arms and made the scariest face he knew how to make. The lazy dog just looked up and yawned. Then it went back to sleep.

"This house is not for me," Tiny muttered.

Tiny looked around some more. He wondered what the perfect place for him would be.

"I guess I need a spooky place that's small," Tiny thought. "And some tiny folks to scare, too."

Tiny had no idea where to look for a place like that. He flew through a park. There were some bees gathering around their hive.

"Everyone's afraid of beehives," he thought. "That just might be the right place for me!"

Maybe Tiny would be big and scary to a teeny-weeny bug. He tried his best to scare the bees there. He walked right in and shouted, "BOO!"

When the bees saw Tiny inside their house, they weren't very happy about it. They kicked him right out.

Those bees weren't afraid of anything! But Tiny was very afraid of them!

"Oh, this house is not right for me!" said Tiny.

Tiny wandered around some more. He had no place to call his own haunted home.

It was getting late. Tiny thought he might have to sleep outside in the rain. He could find a cemetery to sleep in, but there he'd have no one to scare but other ghosts.

Then Tiny spotted his dream house! It wasn't cold and damp, but it was tiny like Tiny.

"This little house just might be the right haunted house for me!" he squealed.

Tiny moved in right away.

"This house needs a lot of work," Tiny huffed. He stayed up all night putting dust in the attic. Tiny hung some cobwebs and dirty, old curtains. He invited some spiders to share the house with him. Soon Tiny's little haunted house was as spooky as could be!

The dolls who lived there looked scary, but they were never scared. They were always happy, even in the spookiest outfits! Tiny still needed someone to scare before he could say he wanted to stay.

The next day Tiny heard some voices near his new house. He crept over to his attic window and peeked outside.

The toy store had filled up with lots of children. Many of the children were bustling around outside Tiny's window!

"Children are easy to scare," Tiny giggled. "I think I'll like it here."

Some of the children walked right up to Tiny's house and looked inside. It was the perfect time for Tiny to do his thing.

Tiny popped out the window. He made a scary face, then he roared out a "BOO!" None of the children expected to see a ghost in the toy store!

"EEEK!" the children shrieked. They were very surprised, and so was Tiny.

"They're afraid of me!" he howled.

Everyone at the store wanted to take a look at Tiny's spooky little haunted home. Every time they did, Tiny popped out. Tiny scared a lot of people that day.

"Yes, indeed!" Tiny said. "This little house just must be the right haunted house for me!"

Counting Sheep

Illustrated by Kathy Wilburn

Written by Catherine McCafferty

Adapted by Brian Conway

Fleecy was a young lamb who was full of energy. She romped through the meadows every day. And she could run and play all day long.

The crickets and butterflies let her chase them through the fields. None of the other sheep could keep up with the little insects. But pouncing, prancing Fleecy surely could. She never wore out.

At the end of the day, Fleecy's friends would fly away. Fleecy wished she could fly like the crickets and butterflies. She looked at the sky as a wonderful, magical place. Fleecy spent each night staring at it.

Fleecy really thought that someday she might take to the sky and fly. The lively little lamb got so wrapped up in her thoughts some nights, she was just about ready to jump right out of her fleece and up to the stars. Fleecy had so much energy that she stayed awake even when it was time to sleep.

Fleecy's mother began to worry about her. "It's not good for a little lamb to stay up so late," her mother told her one night. "A growing lamb needs her sleep."

"I'd like to dream and be awake at the same time, Mom," Fleecy said.

Fleecy's mother had an idea. She knew of Fleecy's fondness for the sky. "Look up to the sky," she said, "and count the stars you see. I'm sure you'll fall asleep soon."

Fleecy gazed at the bright stars in the night sky. She imagined she was high above the field, flying among them. In her dream, she sailed from star to brilliant star, tapping each one as she counted it.

"One, two, three," Fleecy counted. She only got to three before she slipped into sleep.

Fleecy's mother was right. Fleecy slept so well that she had more energy than ever the next day.

"I flew higher than a butterfly in my dream last night," she told her friends as she chased them through the field. "I even touched the stars!"

That night when it was time for sleep, there were no stars to count. Fleecy was very disappointed. She hoped to fly in her dreams and touch many more stars this time.

Again, Fleecy could not sleep. Even after a busy day with the butterflies, Fleecy was still full of energy.

Fleecy's mother noticed the little lamb's restlessness. "Try counting the clouds tonight, dear," said Fleecy's mother. "That should help you get to sleep."

Fleecy watched the clouds slowly crossing the night sky. She imagined she was with them, high above the field. In her dream, she jumped and flew from cloud to cloud. To Fleecy every cloud was a soft, cool pillow puff that wrapped gently around her.

"One, two, three," she counted as she hopped among the clouds. Fleecy only got to three before she was fast asleep.

Sure enough, Fleecy's mother was right again! Counting the clouds really did help Fleecy fall asleep. Once again Fleecy was full of energy for another busy day.

"Last night I hopped from cloud to cloud," Fleecy told her friends in the meadow. "Tonight I'll fly to the clouds at the tippety-top of the sky!"

But the next night there were no clouds. There weren't any stars, either.

"How will I get to sleep now?" Fleecy asked her mother.

Fleecy's mother thought for a moment, then she said, "Try counting the sheep. We'll always be here."

Fleecy started counting all the sheep sleeping in the field. She imagined she floated high above the field, and the sleeping sheep rose up with her as she counted them. In her dream, every sheep's white woolly coat was a puffy cloud on the dark night sky.

"One, two, three," she counted as she floated.

Fleecy only got to three before she was sleeping soundly, just like the rest of the sheep.

From then on, Fleecy's mother never had to worry about her restlessness. That's because Fleecy counted sheep every night. She imagined she was a woolly cloud rising up to the sky, and she counted as the other sheep rose from the field to join her in her dream.

"One, two, three," she counted as she dozed off.

Each night Fleecy only got to three before she was fast asleep. She always slept well, dreaming that she was floating restfully among the soft, puffy clouds.

And Fleecy always had lots of energy in the daytime, too. "I floated to the tippety-top of the sky last night," she told the insects while she chased them. "And someday I'll fly just like you!"

Though she tried again and again, Fleecy was never able to fly like her friends in the meadow did. But in her starry dreams she came closer to flying than any little lamb had ever known.

Little Ant
Goes to School

Illustrated by Richard Bernal

Written by Brian Conway

Little Andy Ant used to spend each day with his pull toy, happily playing outside in the warm summer sun. Then, as the summer days got shorter, the sun didn't feel so warm anymore.

"Summer is over," Andy's mother told him. "That means today is your first day of school!"

Andy had heard about school. He didn't want to be cooped up inside all day long.

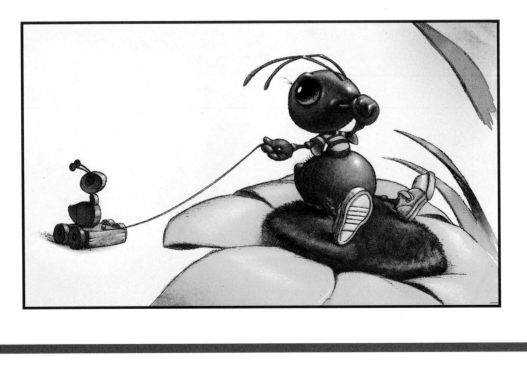

School was a strange, new place. Little Andy Ant wasn't ready to go.

"Can I take my toy along with me?" Andy asked.

"School is for children," his mother answered, "not for toys."

Little Andy Ant tried to be brave. His mother walked him to school that day.

"Maybe school won't be so bad," she said, "once you give it a try." So Andy agreed to try school for just one day.

At school Andy had his very own desk. And he had never seen so many busy little ants bustling around in one place!

Teacher gave the children lots of things to do. Everybody got their own paper and pens! Then they learned about reading and writing.

"You know how ants work together to make anthills?" Andy asked the teacher. "I think letters work together the same way to make words."

Teacher said Andy was right! He was pretty good at drawing and painting and numbers, too!

Little Andy Ant strolled home from school after a long day. Learning new things was fun, and reading and writing were pretty cool, too.

"Maybe you were right," Little Andy Ant told his mother. "Maybe school's not so bad after all."

Andy decided to try school for one more day. The morning passed by quickly for him. Before Andy knew it, it was lunchtime already!

Andy followed the other children to the lunchroom. They got pretty wild there, so Andy sat off to the side, away from all the noise.

Then Lunch Lady called out, "Cookies and milk!"

What a commotion that caused! Little Andy Ant squeezed his way through and got one tiny chunk of cookie. Then he knew what all the fuss was about. Lunch Lady made the best cookies Andy had ever tasted!

Andy trotted home from school. Lunchtime was a pleasant break, and Lunch Lady's cookies were especially good!

"Maybe you were right, Mom," said Little Andy Ant. "Maybe school's not so bad after all."

Andy thought he'd try school for another day. As soon as Andy got there, Teacher said they were going to the woods for a field trip. Andy learned about new plants and berries at every turn!

Some older children made a campfire with their teacher. They needed Andy's help.

"I know how to find the best twigs!" Andy said. He whistled for his friend Tweeter Bird.

Tweeter Bird brought back the finest twigs in the woods. There were enough twigs to build a campfire and for each little ant to roast a marshmallow. All the children at school liked Andy and his friend Tweeter very much.

Andy happily hopped home from school that day. Sitting in those tiny desks was just fine as long as they had field trips and recess, too!

"Maybe you were right, Mom," said Little Andy Ant. "Maybe school's not so bad after all."

The next day, Andy wanted to try school again. He didn't know what to expect in school that day, but he had an idea it might be fun.

"I wonder what will happen today?" Andy thought aloud.

Little Andy Ant sat down at his desk. One of the children whispered, "Please come to my birthday party today."

Andy ran home that day. Up until then, Andy thought birthdays only happened once a year. Now he learned he could celebrate his birthday *and* his friends' birthdays, too!

"I think you were right, Mom," said Little Andy Ant. "Maybe school's not so bad after all."

Andy had fun at his school friend's party. He ate some delicious birthday cake and even got seconds!

Little Andy Ant couldn't wait to get to school the next

day! He hoped it was somebody else's birthday. And he wanted to learn how to count up to real big numbers, like how many birthdays his class would have.

Andy made up a new outside game for his friends that day at recess. Everybody loved to swing and dive! They looked up to Andy as the most adventurous ant in their class.

"You're the best, Andy!" the children shouted.

Little Andy Ant rushed home from school after another fun day. He was so excited.

"You were right, Mom," said Little Andy Ant. "School's not so bad at all. In fact, it's great!"

Little Red Hen

Illustrated by Tammie Speer-Lyon

Adapted by David Presser

Little Red Hen lived on a farm with her three chicks. They lived a simple life and helped each other when there was work to be done. On the farm there also lived a dog, a cat, a mouse, and a horse. They were all happy together. But when the time came to do the chores, the other animals never seemed to lend a hand.

One spring day, Little Red Hen found some seeds and put them into a pail. She went to the field to plant them.

When she got there, Little Red Hen found the dog in his doghouse. He was sleeping.

"Who will help me plant these seeds?" asked Little Red Hen.

"Not I," said the dog as he yawned and stretched.

"Then I will do it myself," said Little Red Hen.

Little Red Hen began planting the seeds in a neat row. Before long, her three chicks came by.

"We will help you," chirped the chicks.

The chicks went to work with their mother. They scratched the ground with their feet and pecked out holes for the seeds.

By the end of the day, they had planted every last seed. After all their hard work, Little Red Hen and her chicks enjoyed the best night's sleep they ever had.

Several busy months passed for Little Red Hen and her chicks. Before they knew it, autumn had arrived.

After months of careful tending, the seeds they had planted in the spring grew into tall, slender stalks of wheat. Little Red Hen and her three chicks took their cart to the field to harvest the wheat.

When they got there, Little Red Hen and her chicks found the cat in the field. The cat was licking her paws.

"Who will help me harvest all this wheat?" asked Little Red Hen.

"Not I," said the cat as she swished her tail back and forth.

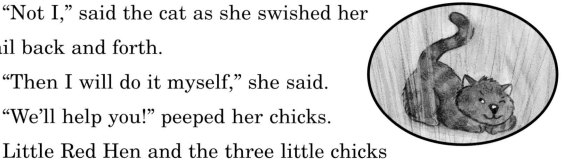

"Then I will do it myself," she said.

"We'll help you!" peeped her chicks.

Little Red Hen and the three little chicks harvested the wheat all by themselves. The cat sat by and watched. By the end of the day, they had a whole cart full of wheat.

The next day, Little Red Hen and her chicks took their cart to the mill. Little Red Hen pulled the cart, while her little chicks pushed from behind with all their might.

Slowly, but surely, they got to the mill and had their wheat made into flour. There were so many bags of flour that their cart was filled to the top.

Little Red Hen and her chicks brought the cart back to the farm, where they found the horse standing in the barn. He was munching on some oats and swatting flies off of his strong back with his tail.

"Who will help me unload this flour?" asked Little Red Hen.

"Not I," said the horse as he munched.

"Then I will do it myself," said Little Red Hen.

"We'll help you," chirped the chicks.

Little Red Hen and her three chicks unloaded the flour, bag by bag, into the barn. It was hard work for such little chicks, but it was fun working together. By the end of the day, they had unloaded all the bags.

In the morning, Little Red Hen and her chicks mixed some of the flour in a big bowl to make dough. When Little Red Hen looked in the cupboard for some sugar, she found the mouse lying about.

"Who will help me make the bread?" asked Little Red Hen.

"Not I," said the mouse as he rolled onto his side.

"Then I will make it myself," said Little Red Hen.

"We'll help you," peeped her chicks.

They all took turns mixing the dough. Then they kneaded it into the shape of a loaf and put it into the oven to bake.

Outside in the yard, the wonderful smell of the baking bread drifted over to the other animals. The dog, the cat, the horse, and the mouse all came to the window of Little Red Hen's kitchen. The bread smelled so good!

When the bread was baked, Little Red Hen took it out of the oven and put it on the table. It looked as delicious as it smelled!

"Who will help me eat this bread?" asked Little Red Hen.

"We will!" said the dog, the cat, the horse, and the mouse.

"Anyone who helped me plant seeds or harvest wheat or unload flour or make dough can help me eat the bread," said Little Red Hen.

The dog, the cat, the horse, and the mouse stood there sadly. But the three chicks danced around.

"We helped you!" chirped the chicks. Then Little Red Hen and her chicks ate the best bread they ever had!

Butterfly Doctor

Illustrated by Mary Lou Faltico

Written by Sarah Toast

Adapted by Lisa Harkrader

D r. Butterfly was the busiest bug in town. "I spend so much time at my office," said Dr. Butterfly, "that I don't have much time to play with my own son." She snapped her fingers. "I know what I'll do. I'll take Billy to work with me."

When Dr. Butterfly and Billy Butterfly arrived at the office, Nurse Nita was busy answering phones. Dr. Butterfly looked at all the names written in the appointment book. Then Dr. Butterfly looked at the crowded waiting room. It was full of patients.

"Another busy day," she said.

Dr. Butterfly found a place in the waiting room for Billy and his toy bug. "You play here," she told Billy. "I'll be back out soon."

Dr. Butterfly hurried into the examining room to see her first two patients, Annie and Archie Ant. They were twins, and they needed a checkup for school.

Nurse Nita checked Annie's reflexes while Dr. Butterfly weighed and measured Archie. Then Dr. Butterfly looked in the twins' ears, throats, and noses with a little light. She listened to their hearts with her stethoscope.

"You're in perfect health," she told them.

Dr. Butterfly's next patient was Calvin Cricket, the town's chief mechanic. "I have a terrible headache," said Calvin, "and it won't go away."

"Let me take a look," said Dr. Butterfly. But it didn't take her long to figure out what was wrong.

"I have good news and bad news," said Dr. Butterfly. "The good news is you won't need a shot or a pill or an X ray."

"That is good news," said Calvin. "What's the bad news?"

"The bad news," said Dr. Butterfly, "is that you have your best wrench stuck in your antennas, and you won't be able to fix anyone's car until I get it out."

Calvin patted the top of his head. "So that's where my wrench went," he said. "I thought it was lost."

Calvin sat very still on the examining table while Dr. Butterfly untangled the wrench from his antennas. When it was finally loose, Calvin went back to his garage, and Dr. Butterfly called in her next patient.

"Mom, wait!" called Billy. "I need to show you something."

"In a minute, dear," said Dr. Butterfly. "I'm very busy at the moment."

Dr. Butterfly looked at all the patients she still needed to see. Mr. and Mrs. Dragonfly brought in their baby, Daisy, for her shots. Teddy Termite had chicken pox, and Curtis Caterpillar had come down with the flu.

"I'll be with you as soon as I can," Dr. Butterfly told Billy. "Right now I have a waiting room full of patients who need my help."

"I need your help, too," said Billy.

But his mother didn't hear him. She had already taken her next patient into her office and closed the door.

Dr. Butterfly gave Daisy Dragonfly her shots. She gave Teddy Termite medicine to make him feel better. She took Curtis Caterpillar's temperature, gave him an aspirin, and told him to get plenty of sleep.

Then Dr. Butterfly rushed over to Billy. "Now, what did you want to show me?" she asked.

"It's my toy bug," said Billy. But before Billy could say anything more, Nurse Nita hurried into the waiting room.

"Dr. Butterfly, come quick," she said. "Sammy Spider fell from his web. I think he broke his leg."

Dr. Butterfly hurried into the examining room to take an X ray of Sammy's leg. "It's broken, all right," she said.

Nurse Nita helped Dr. Butterfly put a cast on Sammy's leg. Then Dr. Butterfly showed Sammy how to use his crutches.

"It will take some time," Dr. Butterfly told him, "but your leg will heal just fine. You'll be spinning new webs all over town in no time."

Nurse Nita and Dr. Butterfly waved good-bye as Sammy hobbled out the door on his crutches. Then she turned and glanced around the waiting room.

"Was Sammy the last patient?" she asked Nurse Nita. "Have we already taken care of everyone else?"

"No, there's one more," said Billy as he held up his toy bug. One of the bug's seams had torn open. And its stuffing was starting to fall out. "Mom, can you fix my toy bug like you fixed all the other bugs?" he asked.

She smiled. "I can certainly try."

Dr. Butterfly carried Billy's toy bug into the examining room. She took the bug's temperature and listened to its heart. She looked into its ears and nose and throat with her little light. Then she put a bandage over its torn seam.

"Good as new," said Dr. Butterfly.

Billy gave his mother a big hug. "You take very good care of everyone in town," he said. "Especially me."

Baby Calf

Illustrated by Erin Mauterer

Written by Catherine McCafferty

Adapted by Sarah Toast

Clover was a little calf. She lived with some other cows and calves on a farm. The farm had a big pasture with plenty of sweet green grass to eat.

There was so much grassy land that all of the cows had their own eating spots. Clover's favorite place was the patch of grass by the big gray rock.

"The grass here is so good," she thought. "It must be the sweetest grass in the whole field."

A little ground squirrel lived in a burrow under the gray rock. He didn't like Clover eating so close to his home, because he didn't like the sound of her bell. It clanged whenever Clover strolled from one tuft of grass to another. The ground squirrel covered his ears, but it never helped.

One day the ground squirrel thought of a plan. "How do you know that the grass by the gray rock is the sweetest grass in the pasture?" he asked Clover.

"I know that I like it very much," she said.

"Let me tell you a little secret," the ground squirrel whispered. "I have heard that the grass on the hillside is really the best-tasting grass of all."

Clover looked at the hillside, where another calf, Daisy, was eating in her favorite spot. Daisy looked happy munching on some posies.

"Her grass does look greener and sweeter," said Clover. "Why don't I pay her a visit."

Clover walked over to Daisy's flower patch. "Hello, Daisy," she said. "May I have a nibble of your grass?"

"Of course," said Daisy.

Clover had a nibble and smiled. The grass seemed so good that Clover took another bite, then another and another. Soon Clover helped herself to all of the grass.

"That ground squirrel was right," said Clover. "This grass is the best-tasting grass of all."

Clover kept on eating, which didn't make Daisy happy. But what could Daisy do?

Finally Clover took a break from eating and looked up. She saw Lily eating in her favorite spot by the fence. Lily looked really happy. Her grass also looked greener and sweeter than Daisy's.

"I think I'll pay Lily a visit," Clover said.

Clover trotted over to the fence where Lily ate. "Hello, Lily," she said. "May I have a nibble of your grass?"

"Sure," said Lily.

Clover had a nibble and grinned from ear to ear. The grass seemed so very sweet that Clover took another bite, then another and another. Soon Clover helped herself to all the grass in sight!

"This grass seems even better than Daisy's," said Clover. "This grass is the best-tasting grass of all."

Clover kept on eating, which didn't make Lily happy. But Lily knew just what to do. She left Clover by the fence and went off to find Sweetheart, the wisest cow in the field.

Lily walked to Sweetheart's favorite spot on the other side of the pasture. Sure enough, Lily found Sweetheart and her friend Daisy was there, too!

"It's so nice to see the both of you on this fine day," said Sweetheart. "What brings you here for a visit?"

"I was hoping you could help me," said Daisy. "I was eating the grass in my flower patch, when Clover came over and ate and ate and ate."

"Then she came over to my patch," said Lily. "And she's eating there now."

"I think I know the problem," said Sweetheart. "Clover doesn't know that the grass in her patch is just as sweet and good as any grass in the pasture."

Sweetheart walked through the field to Lily's patch by the fence. There she found Clover, who was still eating.

"Hello, Clover," she said. "Are you enjoying the grass?"

Clover nodded yes, as she munched.

"Would you like to taste grass as sweet as any in the whole pasture?" Sweetheart asked kindly.

"Oh, yes!" said Clover.

"Well, close your eyes, dear, and I'll lead you to it."

Clover closed her eyes and followed the sound of Sweetheart's bell. They walked for a bit, until Sweetheart said, "This is the place."

Clover kept her eyes closed and munched the grass where she stood. "This grass is so-o-o delicious!" said Clover.

"Open your eyes, dear," said Sweetheart. "This is your own patch!"

Clover couldn't believe it. She opened her eyes and saw that it was her favorite spot by the big gray rock. "This is a great place to be!" said Clover.

When the ground squirrel heard Clover talking, he hurried out of his burrow. The gray rock had been lonely without her and the sound of her bell. "It *is* a great place to be," he chimed in. "And I have heard that the grass by the gray rock is the sweetest grass in the pasture."

Fox and Poodle Together

Illustrated by Don Sullivan

Written by Brian Conway

Frankie Fox and Penelope Poodle were a great team. Together, they had the best magic act in the whole world. Everyone marveled at the amazing tricks they could do, and to this very day, nobody's really sure how they did them.

Frankie and Penelope liked to share their wonderful magic with everyone, so they traveled from town to town to put on their show.

They'd been to many different places all over the globe, but they'd never had a place to call home. Now Frankie and Penelope wanted to find the one perfect place where they could live for the rest of their lives.

They came upon a quiet little farm town. "This looks like a nice place," Frankie said.

Penelope agreed, adding, "If they like our show, perhaps we'll stay."

That very night, all the farmers in town showed up to see Frankie and Penelope's magic show at the old town hall. They waited in excited silence to see the most extraordinary and fantastic things.

"I, The Great Frankini," Frankie called, "have a special surprise for you. Tonight, you'll see our greatest trick first."

Penelope shook her head. "No, no," she whispered, "not that one, Frankie."

Frankie called to the crowd, "My assistant thinks I should start with a card trick, but you deserve the best, don't you?"

The farmers agreed with lots of claps, hoots, and hollers. Frankie showed them his magic hat. It was dark and empty inside. He twirled his magic wand, tapped the hat three times, reached in, and pulled out a fuzzy, little white rabbit!

The crowd roared. The rabbit trick worked every time.

Frankie really wanted to impress his new neighbors. He tapped the hat again, and another rabbit popped out! It made the farmers laugh, so Frankie made another rabbit appear, and another, and another!

Soon the town hall was crawling with bouncing bunnies! The rabbits hopped out the door and hurried into the fields.

Then the farmers stopped laughing. They booed and hissed at the two magicians.

Frankie was confused as Penelope pulled the trunk away to make a hasty exit. The Great Frankini took a quick bow and followed her.

"Get outta here, and take your magic with you," the farmers yelled. "Those rabbits will eat our crops!"

So Frankie and Penelope left that town. Their last trick there was a disappearing act!

Frankie and Penelope rowed a boat to a new land. "Will we ever find a place to call home?" Penelope sighed.

"I'm sure we will," Frankie assured her.

"The folks there will be really cool," Penelope said. "We'll like them, and they'll like us."

"And they'll love our funny kind of magic," Frankie added.

As the two lonely magicians hoped and dreamed of their perfect place, they rowed to the next shore. They landed on a tiny island that Frankie couldn't find on a map.

They didn't see a single soul on the island, but Penelope noticed a lot of pawprints scattered about the sunny, sandy shore. They looked around through lush grasses and tall trees, cool streams and green fields.

"This would be paradise," said Penelope, "if only we had an audience."

"The best way to get an audience," said Frankie, "is to put on a show!"

Frankie and Penelope set up a simple stage in a field. Then they started their show.

"Ladies and Gentlemen," Penelope announced. "Allow me to present The Great Frankini!"

The magicians stood there in the middle of the field and performed their spinning dish trick. They heard some rustling in the field. Then The Great Frankini made a dove appear from beneath his magic scarf, and a few furry heads popped up from the tall grass. Some shy island cats came to see their magic show!

Then Frankie changed his crummy old sneakers into a pair of fancy shoes, and a whole crowd of cats came closer to the stage. They smiled and mewed for more magic fun!

Those island cats had never seen magic before. They were astounded! It was the best show they'd ever seen!

Frankie and Penelope agreed that these cats were the best audience they'd ever had, too. The cats were so grateful, they decided to put on a little show of their own.

The show began, and this time, Frankie and Penelope were the audience! The magicians laughed and sang and played along. They spent a great day on the beach with the cats.

"We wish you and your wonderful magic could stay here with us," the cats purred.

Frankie and Penelope were thinking the very same thing! These great magicians didn't need any magic to grant that wish! They finally found the perfect place to call home.

Brave Little Bulldozer

Illustrated by Jim Talbot

Written by Tom Lynch

Adapted by Brian Conway

Buster Bulldozer was always the first truck on the construction site. Every morning just as the sun came out, he revved up his motor and started working before any of the other trucks got moving.

"Vrrrooom!" Buster Bulldozer roared his engine. "Let's go, everybody! We have a building to build!"

Buster was just a little bulldozer, but he had a very big job to do. He had to keep the site smooth and safe for all the other trucks.

Buster Bulldozer had a special blade for pushing heavy dirt and debris around the site. He cleared the way for the bigger cranes and dump trucks.

Nobody wanted an accident to happen. The other trucks knew they'd be safe when Buster Bulldozer was on the job!

One day, the foreman called on Buster. "I have a new job for you to do today," he told Buster. "We need a whole lot of dirt ready at the edge of the ditch."

Usually the bigger bulldozers took care of that job. Little Buster Bulldozer wasn't sure he could do it all by himself. And besides, who would keep the site safe?

"Don't worry about it today, Buster," said the foreman hurriedly. "We're counting on you to get the fill dirt ready."

Buster pushed and pushed to make big dirt piles at the edge of the new building. His engine ran louder than ever. He knew the other trucks were counting on him.

"You're pretty strong for your size, Buster," said Rusty Roller, the oldest truck on the site. "Just move a little faster."

Suddenly Buster and Rusty heard a booming crash coming from inside the ditch. Buster hoped it wasn't an accident, but he expected the worst. "What could that be?" he asked.

"Help!" cried Clumsy Crane. "I'm stuck!"

Buster Bulldozer had been too busy to keep the site safe. He hoped the accident was not his fault.

"What happened?" Buster called back.

"My platform broke suddenly," Clumsy answered, "and I fell into the ditch!"

A big crane like Clumsy could not work his way out of a deep ditch. He needed a truck with a lot of pulling power!

Buster Bulldozer had a lot of pushing power, but he was not too sure he could handle this emergency pulling job. He called down to Clumsy anyway. "I can help!" Buster said.

Then Tuffy Tow Truck zoomed onto the scene. Tuffy's wide, whirring tires kicked up lots of dust and dirt.

"Move over, little guy," said Tuffy as he drove past Buster. "I'll take care of this mess."

Buster felt just terrible. What could he do to help now?

Tuffy tried to pull Clumsy Crane out of the ditch. A heavy crane is usually easy for a tough truck like Tuffy to pull, but not this time. The ditch was so deep, Tuffy began to slip.

Buster watched helplessly as Tuffy tried and tried again. Tuffy's engine roared, and his wheels were spinning in the soft dirt. Clumsy Crane would not budge, and Tuffy kept slipping and sliding down the steep hill. Then both of them were trapped! "What are we going to do now?" asked Clumsy.

Even with all his pushing power and special dirt treads, Buster Bulldozer could not pull a crane and a tow truck up that huge dirt hill. He didn't know what to do either.

But all the other trucks at the site were counting on Buster Bulldozer to come through. So brave little Buster came up with a very different kind of plan.

"Don't worry," Buster said to Clumsy and Tuffy. "I'll help you drive right out of there."

Buster Bulldozer knew he couldn't pull them out, but maybe he could clear a path at the edge of the ditch. If the big hill was gone, Buster thought, so was their problem.

Buster Bulldozer pushed the dirt to the side, pile after pile. That was Buster's special skill, after all, and Buster was the only truck who could help now. With every load of dirt he pushed, the hill got smaller and smaller.

Buster Bulldozer worked very quickly. "Go, Buster, go!" shouted the other trucks. "You can do it!"

Before long the huge hill was gone. Buster cleared a smooth, easy path for Tuffy Tow Truck and Clumsy Crane.

When Clumsy and Tuffy drove out, everybody cheered.

"Thanks, Buster Bulldozer," said Tuffy Tow Truck. "I didn't think a little guy like you could do it."

"You saved us!" said Clumsy Crane. "You're smart and strong and very brave."

From that day on, all the trucks at the construction site knew they could count on Buster. They never worried about accidents again, as long as Buster Bulldozer was on the job!

Little Squeak

Illustrated by Richard Bernal

Written by Sarah Toast

Adapted by Megan Musgrave

Once there was a very small mouse named Little Squeak who lived in a great big house. She had a very nice, cozy mouse hole in one corner of the children's playroom. She loved to sit quietly in the doorway of her mouse hole and watch the little boy and girl playing with their toys.

"Look at all those wonderful toys!" thought Little Squeak as she watched the children playing. "How I would love to play with them myself!"

One night, Little Squeak decided to have a closer look at the toys. She waited until the children were tucked into bed,

and then she crept quietly into the playroom. At that moment, a wonderful thing happened. The shining moon in the window lit up the room and brought all of the toys to life.

"Come and play with us, Little Squeak!" called the toys.

Little Squeak was so excited. But she didn't know where to begin.

"I wonder which one will be my favorite toy!" she squeaked.

"Little Squeak, come play with me!" cried the red rubber ball. "I can bounce and bound all over the playroom!"

Little Squeak jumped on top of the ball and rode it around the room. "Boing, boing!" went the ball. It was very exciting, but after a little while all of the bouncing began to make Little Squeak dizzy.

"Thank you, Ball, but I'm looking for something a little less bouncy," said Little Squeak politely.

Little Squeak hopped off the ball and scurried over to the toy chest. She peeked inside and found a big robot.

"Come march with me, Little Squeak!" said the bright blue robot as he climbed out of the toy chest. "I can clang and clatter all day long!"

Little Squeak stuck out her arms and straightened her legs and marched across the playroom with the robot. But soon her arms and legs became too stiff and straight.

"Thank you, Robot, but sometimes I like to twirl and whirl," said Little Squeak.

Little Squeak spied some musical instruments in the corner. She jingled the tambourine and tapped on the drum.

"Come make music with me, Little Squeak!" called the brightly colored xylophone.

Little Squeak hopped up onto the xylophone. First she jumped onto a yellow key, "Ding!" Then she hopped onto a green key, "Dong!" Soon Little Squeak was whirling and twirling and dancing all over the colorful keys.

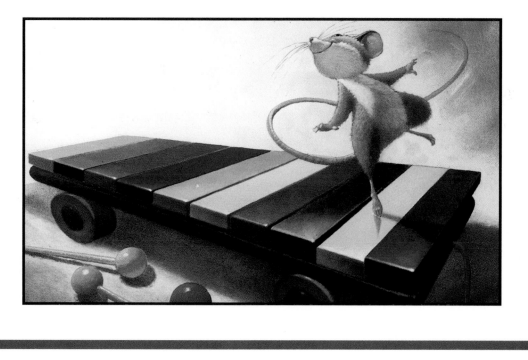

Little Squeak hummed and sang while the xylophone played along. What a lovely tune they made! But after a while, Little Squeak's tiny feet began to get tired.

"Making music is hard work!" panted Little Squeak. "Thank you, Xylophone, but I need a rest!"

Just then, the toy bug zoomed up beside her. "Come along for a ride with me, Little Squeak!"

Little Squeak hopped onto the back of the toy bug. "Hold on tight!" cried the bug as it took off across the room.

"Yippee!" Little Squeak shouted as they zipped under the teatime table and around the doll house.

"Vrroom!" said the toy bug as it bounced over the train tracks and scooted across the play-castle bridge. After a wild ride, the toy bug skidded to a stop right in front of the airplane hangar. Little Squeak slid down from the bug.

"Thank you, Toy Bug, but I'm looking for something a little less bumpy," said Little Squeak.

Little Squeak heard a buzz and a whir. The noises came from inside the airplane hangar.

"Why don't you come fly with me, Little Squeak?" called a voice from inside the hangar. Out puttered the shiny new jet plane. Little Squeak climbed into the pilot's seat.

"Up, up, and away!" she cried. Little Squeak and the jet plane sped across the floor and lifted off the ground.

"Whee!" shouted Little Squeak. The jet plane flew high above the other toys and circled around the playroom. Little Squeak looked down and saw the doll waving at her from the doll house window.

"Hello, down there!" called Little Squeak.

Just then, Little Squeak heard someone coming up the stairs. The children had finished breakfast, and they were coming up to say good morning to their toys.

"Time to go home, Jet Plane!" said Little Squeak. The jet plane landed right beside Little Squeak's front door.

"Good-bye, everyone!" Little Squeak called to the toys.

"Good-bye, Little Squeak! Come and play again tomorrow!" they answered.

Little Squeak scurried back into her mouse hole just as the children came into the playroom. "I hope our toys aren't lonely when we're not here," they said.

"Don't worry!" Little Squeak wanted to tell the children. "Your toys will never be lonely with me around."

Thumbelina

Illustrated by Bryn Bernard

Adapted by Megan Musgrave

There was once a woman who lived in a cottage with a beautiful garden. One day she found a golden ring among the flowers.

"What a beautiful ring!" exclaimed the woman. She didn't know that it was really a magical crown, lost by a fairy who once visited her garden.

The woman put the ring on her finger. Suddenly a new tulip bloomed in the flower patch. Its pretty petals opened and there sat a tiny girl, hardly as big as a thumb. She wore a buttercup for a dress and had long golden hair.

"You are the most beautiful child I've ever seen! Would

you like to live with me in my cottage?" asked the woman.

"Oh, yes!" replied the tiny girl.

"Then I will call you Thumbelina," said the woman. They lived together very happily.

One evening, a frog hopped through the garden. He heard Thumbelina singing by the pond.

When the frog saw the tiny girl, he said, "I have never seen or heard such a beautiful creature! I must take her away to be my wife."

The frog waited until Thumbelina's mother went inside. Then he jumped out from behind the reeds and captured Thumbelina. The frog carried her away to his lily pad on the river.

"Rest here while I go and make plans for our wedding," said the frog. With that, he hopped away.

"I don't want to be the wife of a frog," said Thumbelina. Thumbelina became so sad that she began to cry.

A fish in the river heard her crying. "I'll help you," said the kind fish.

"But how?" Thumbelina asked.

The fish nibbled through the stem of her lily pad until it broke free. The lily pad floated down the river.

"Thank you," said Thumbelina as she sailed far away.

Soon the lily pad came to rest on a grassy bank of the river. Thumbelina climbed up the bank and found herself on the edge of a meadow.

"This will be a fine place for me to live," said Thumbelina.

Soon the days began to grow cold. The meadow was covered in snow.

"How will I keep warm in the winter?" cried Thumbelina.

A field mouse who lived nearby heard Thumbelina. The field mouse was always happy to have visitors.

"Come into my burrow!" said the field mouse. "Come sit by the fire and have a warm cup of tea."

Thumbelina and the field mouse soon became close friends. "How would you like to stay with me for the winter?" the field mouse asked.

"I would like that very much," said Thumbelina.

They filled their winter days with storytelling. Thumbelina loved the field mouse's stories of fairy princes and princesses.

One day Thumbelina peeked out of the burrow. She found a young swallow with a broken wing lying on the ground nearby. Thumbelina helped the swallow down into the cozy warm burrow.

"I surely would have frozen to death if you hadn't found me," chirped the swallow.

All winter long, Thumbelina took care of the swallow. She fed him warm soup and helped his wing to heal.

One morning Thumbelina poked her head outside the burrow again. The snow was nearly melted, and tiny green shoots appeared all over the meadow.

"Spring is coming!" she shouted to her friends.

The swallow decided it was time to leave. "You saved my life, Thumbelina," he said. "Now I would like to help you."

Thumbelina said good-bye to her field mouse friend, then climbed onto the swallow's back. She held onto his feathers, as they flew off into the sky.

Thumbelina held on tight, as the swallow flew deep into the forest and landed gently in a thicket. Sunlight streamed down from between the trees. All around her, beautiful flowers of every color blossomed.

"This must be a magical place," said Thumbelina, "like the places in the field mouse's stories."

Suddenly, a beautiful lily opened before her. Inside the lily sat a tiny boy, no bigger than a thumb. He had a beautiful pair of silvery wings.

"Who are you?" asked Thumbelina.

"I am the Prince of the Flowers," said the boy. "You are the most beautiful girl I have ever seen. Come and live with us here, and be the Princess of the Flowers."

"Thank you," said Thumbelina. "I would be happy to live here."

With that, the meadow came alive. Tiny fairies stepped out of the flowers.

"These are fit for a princess," said the fairies as they gave Thumbelina a pair of beautiful silvery wings.

All the animals of the forest also came to see the beautiful new princess. Thumbelina stayed with them in the magic thicket, where it was summer all the time and where it never grew cold.

Make Room
for Penny

Illustrated by Lyn Martin

Written by Catherine McCafferty

Adapted by Brian Conway

Every afternoon, when it got too hot to play beside the barn, the mother pigs sent their piglets out to play in their mud puddle by the stream. The puddle was crowded with all the little pigs from the farm.

Penny Piglet was tired of sharing that cramped mud puddle. No matter which way Penny turned, she bumped into someone.

"Excuse me," Penny muttered, squeezing her way into the puddle. "Pardon me, please."

Penny found a little spot at the edge of the puddle. She nudged her way into it, laid down, and rolled onto her side.

"Ah, much better," Penny sighed. "I'll just take a little nap."

Then Patty Piglet decided her belly was too warm. She rolled over and nudged Potter Piglet. Potter moved a little and bumped Percy Piglet, who rolled onto Peggy Piglet. Peggy slipped over. She bumped poor Penny Piglet right out of the puddle!

"That's it!" Penny thought to herself. "I will never be able to take a nap or cool off, unless I have my own mud puddle." With that, she went off to look for the perfect spot.

Penny Piglet decided to make her own mud puddle. She picked a new spot right next to the stream. Penny dug a nook in the shore. It was wide enough so she'd have plenty of room to roll around in any direction she pleased.

Penny rolled around in the fresh mud. She spread out like she never could before. But Penny was no longer sleepy.

She wanted to play! Penny did a belly-slide and splashed a lot of mud, but no one was there to splash her back.

Penny had room in her puddle for a friend. She decided to let Percy Piglet play with her, but only Percy, no one else.

Penny and Percy had lots of fun splashing. The fresh new mud was perfect for diving and spinning and slipping and sliding. With Penny and Percy playing together, the mud was really flying!

"Let's play piggy-in-the-middle," said Percy. That was Percy's favorite game!

Penny liked playing piggy-in-the-middle, too. "We can try," said Penny.

She got a stick, and they tried to keep it away from each other. That was very hard to do with only two pigs in the puddle. Soon they figured out they couldn't play this game with only two of them.

"Penny, we have plenty of room," Percy said. "I think there's enough space for one more friend."

Penny thought it would be okay for another friend to join them. They called Peggy Piglet to come by and play in Penny's new puddle.

Piggy-in-the-middle was much better with three of them! They tossed the stick from one friend to another. That was the most fun they'd had in Penny's puddle yet!

"I've never had so much fun playing piggy-in-the middle!" squealed Peggy.

"Neither have we!" Percy and Penny laughed.

There was plenty of room to stomp and flop. It was easy to play piggy-in-the-middle, and Penny didn't have to bump into another piglet unless she wanted to, of course!

Penny wondered if other games would be as much fun in the new puddle. Before long she had a great idea.

"Pig pile!" she shouted.

Pig piles are a piglet's favorite game. They get to topple and tumble all over each other. They start slipping and sliding and piling up.

It's the messiest game a piglet ever plays, too. They get covered in mud from head to tail! That's why piglets love it so much!

Penny tried a pig pile with Percy and Peggy. There wasn't much tumbling going on, and it wasn't that much fun with just three.

"We have plenty of space for more friends," Peggy said. "Let's ask Patty and Potter to play with us."

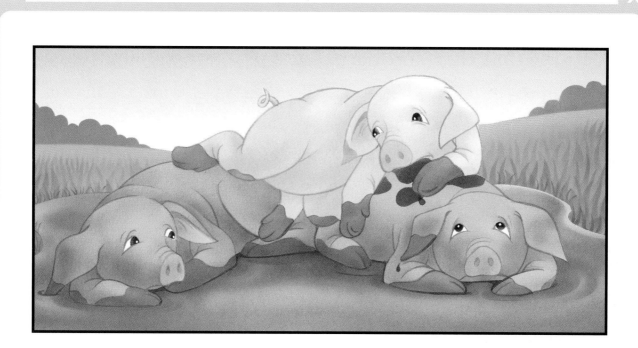

"Our pig pile will be much better if we do!" Percy urged Penny. So Penny asked Patty and Potter to come over and play in her new mud puddle.

"Pig pile!" Penny shouted.

The five playful piglets sloshed happily in the fresh mud. Peggy flopped over Patty! Potter tumbled over Percy! Penny rolled and squeezed her way around them all! They made the muddiest, messiest, splashiest, sloshiest pig pile ever!

By the time they were done, those piglets were wearing most of the mud in the puddle! They couldn't wait to play in that puddle again.

From then on, the piglets rushed to the puddle and jumped in, shouting, "Pig pile!" all the way! And that's just how Penny liked it.

Now Penny's puddle was perfect. Penny Piglet never wanted her own puddle again.

Bugtown Firehouse

Illustrated by Sherry Neidigh

Written by Sarah Toast

Adapted by Lisa Harkrader

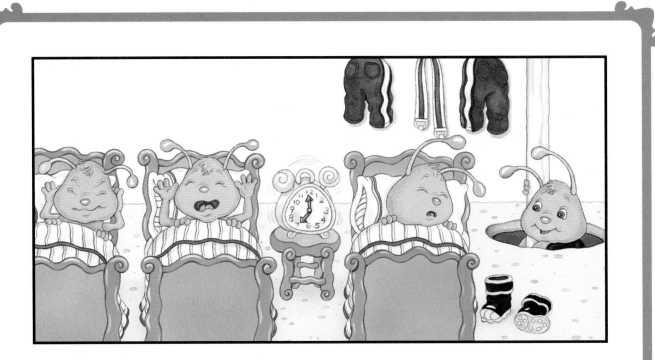

The alarm clock rang early at the Bugtown Firehouse. *Brrring!* The fire beetles yawned and stretched.

"Time to get up," said Baxter Beetle, the fire captain. "The bugs of Bugtown are counting on us to keep them safe. We don't want to let them down."

The beetles hopped out of their warm, cozy beds. They pulled on their fire pants and fire boots. They fastened their suspenders. Then they slid down the fire pole.

Benjy Beetle was the first one down. He was eager to start the day. Benjy was the newest fire beetle, and he wanted to show Captain Baxter how quickly he could dress and line up for the morning roll call. "I'm ready, Captain," said Benjy.

Captain Baxter smiled. "Not so fast, Benjy. Your pants are backwards and your boots are on the wrong feet."

Benjy's cheeks turned red. His antennas drooped. By the time he had turned his pants around and switched his boots, he was the last fire beetle in line! Benjy just shook his head.

After roll call, the beetles started their morning chores. They grabbed water buckets and sponges and sudsed up the fire engine. They scrubbed it and waxed it till it shined.

Then they made sure the fire engine was ready to fight fires. They checked the ladders. They rang the bell and sounded the siren. Then they unrolled the fire hose.

"We need to practice," said Captain Baxter. "When water rushes through the hose, it can be very hard to control."

The fire beetles took turns. They held the hose tight as the water gushed out the nozzle. They practiced aiming the water in different directions, up and down, left and right.

Benjy was excited to take his turn. He had never used the fire hose before. He wanted to do a good job for Captain Baxter. "I'm ready! Turn on the water!" called Benjy.

Benjy held the hose tight. But the water was too powerful. The nozzle twisted this way and that.

Then, even though he didn't mean to, Benjy squirted water all over the freshly waxed fire engine.

"I'm sorry," Benjy said. "I'll polish the engine again."

Captain Baxter patted Benjy on the back. "Don't feel bad. You'll get better with practice. We've worked up an appetite. Let's get some breakfast. You can polish the engine later."

The hungry beetles gathered around the table in the firehouse kitchen. The firehouse cook brought them a pan of freshly baked muffins and set them on the table.

"They look delicious," said the fire beetles.

"Yes," said Captain Baxter, "I'm hungry."

Before the fire beetles could eat the muffins, the phone rang.

Captain Baxter got up and answered it. It was a ladybug who lived at the edge of town. She had looked out her living room window and saw smoke coming from the woods. Captain Baxter wrote down everything she said.

"No time for breakfast," he said. "We have an emergency. We have to put out this fire before it spreads."

The beetles grabbed their fire hats and jumped on board the fire engine. They turned on their siren and rang their bells. *Whirr! Whirr! Clang! Clang! Clang!* The fire engine raced down the streets of Bugtown and through the woods.

"There's the smoke!" shouted Captain Baxter.

The beetles followed the trail of smoke. They even found the fire. But it was not an emergency.

"It's a troop of Bug Scouts," said Captain Baxter. "The smoke is coming from their campfire."

Captain Baxter stopped the fire engine. He wanted to talk to the scouts.

"Sorry you came here for nothing," said the scout leader.

"Don't be sorry," said Captain Baxter. "We like campfires a lot better than forest fires."

"Please stay and have some breakfast," said the leader.

The beetles gathered around the campfire. The scouts handed them plates of bacon and eggs.

"Captain, look!" Benjy pointed to a nearby tree. A baby caterpillar was stuck on one of the top branches.

"I'll climb up the fire ladder and get him," said Benjy.

"Have you ever used a fire ladder before?" asked Captain Baxter. Benjy shook his head. "Then maybe you should let me climb up and get the little fellow." Benjy agreed.

Captain Baxter climbed up to the little caterpillar and held out his arms. The caterpillar held tightly to Captain Baxter, as he safely climbed back down.

"Good job, Benjy!" said Captain Baxter.

Benjy's antennas perked up. "What for?"

"You saw the little guy. You were alert and quick-thinking. You're going to make a very good fire beetle." The captain smiled. "But you still need practice with the fire hose."